Access to History

General Editor: Keith Randell

The USA and the World, 1917-45

Peter Brett

Hodder & Stoughton

A MEMBER OF THE HODDER HEADLINE GROUP

The cover illustration shows an American recruitment poster depicting the attack on Pearl Harbor, reproduced courtesy of the Imperial War Museum.

Some other titles in the series:

Prosperity, Depression and the New Deal　　　ISBN 0 340　65871 1
Peter Clements

The USA and the Cold War　　　ISBN 0 340　67963 8
Oliver Edwards

The Origins of the American Civil War: 1846-61　　　ISBN 0 340　65869 X
Alan Farmer

The American Civil War: 1861-65　　　ISBN 0 340　65870 3
Alan Farmer

British Library Cataloguing in Publication Data

A catalogue for this title is available from the British Library

ISBN 0-340-68351-1

First published 1997

Impression number　　10　9　8　7　6　5　4　3　2　1
Year　　　　　　　　　2000　　1999　　1998　　1997

Typeset by Sempringham publishing services, Bedford
Printed in Great Britain for Hodder & Stoughton Educational,
a division of Hodder Headline Plc, 338 Euston Road, London NW1 3BH by
Redwood Books, Trowbridge, Wiltshire.

Contents

Preface

To the general reader

Although the *Access to History* series has been designed with the needs of students studying the subject at higher examination levels very much in mind, it also has a great deal to offer the general reader. The main body of the text (i.e. ignoring the Study Guides at the ends of chapters) forms a readable and yet stimulating survey of a coherent topic as studied by historians. However, each author's aim has not merely been to provide a clear explanation of what happened in the past (to interest and inform): it has also been assumed that most readers wish to be stimulated into thinking further about the topic and to form opinions of their own about the significance of the events that are described and discussed (to be challenged). Thus, although no prior knowledge of the topic is expected on the reader's part, she or he is treated as an intelligent and thinking person throughout. The author tends to share ideas and possibilities with the reader, rather than passing on numbers of so-called 'historical truths'.

To the student reader

There are many ways in which the series can be used by students studying History at a higher level. It will, therefore, be worthwhile thinking about your own study strategy before you start your work on this book. Obviously, your strategy will vary depending on the aim you have in mind, and the time for study that is available to you.

If, for example, you want to acquire a general overview of the topic in the shortest possible time, the following approach will probably be the most effective:

1 Read Chapter 1 and think about its contents.
2 Read the 'Making notes' section at the end of Chapter 2 and decide whether it is necessary for you to read this chapter.
3 If it is, read the chapter, stopping at each heading to note down the main points that have been made.
4 Repeat stage 2 (and stage 3 where appropriate) for all the other chapters.

If, however, your aim is to gain a thorough grasp of the topic, taking however much time is necessary to do so, you may benefit from carrying out the same procedure with each chapter, as follows:

1 Read the chapter as fast as you can, and preferably at one sitting.
2 Study the flow diagram at the end of the chapter, ensuring that you understand the general 'shape' of what you have just read.

3 Read the 'Making notes' section (and the 'Answering essay questions' section, if there is one) and decide what further work you need to do on the chapter. In particularly important sections of the book, this will involve reading the chapter a second time and stopping at each heading to think about (and to write a summary of) what you have just read.
4 Attempt the 'Source-based questions' section. It will sometimes be sufficient to think through your answers, but additional understanding will often be gained by forcing yourself to write them down.

When you have finished the main chapters of the book, study the 'Further Reading' section and decide what additional reading (if any) you will do on the topic.

This book has been designed to help make your studies both enjoyable and successful. If you can think of ways in which this could have been done more effectively, please write to tell me. In the meantime, I hope that you will gain greatly from your study of History.

Keith Randell

Acknowledgements

The Publishers would like to thank the following for permission to reproduce illustrations in this volume:

Cover - An American recruitment poster depicting the attack on Pearl Harbor, reproduced courtesy of the Imperial War Museum. *Washington Evening Star*, p. 92; Mirror Syndication International, p. 140 (bottom); Low cartoon supplied by Centre for the Study of Cartoon and Caricature, University of Kent at Canterbury p. 140 (top).

Every effort has been made to trace and acknowledge ownership of copyright. The Publishers will be glad to make suitable arrangements with any copyright holders whom it has not been possible to contact.

CHAPTER 1

Introduction: The USA and the World, 1917-45

1 Introduction

On a sunny Sunday in December 1941 the Japanese launched an air attack on Pearl Harbor, a naval base in Hawaii. It came as a bolt out of the blue to almost all Americans. Most people had assumed that Japan lacked the means and the will to risk a direct assault upon the United States. It was on 7 December 1941 at approximately 7.55 am, Hawaii time, that carrier-based Japanese dive-bombers, torpedo planes, and fighters struck at the American fleet and military installations in and around Pearl Harbor. It was the worst naval disaster in American history. The attack on Pearl Harbor produced an immediate and violent reaction in the United States. Diplomatic negotiations with Japan had been in progress and there had been no Japanese declaration of war. American leaders and public opinion were not only shocked at the losses but furiously resentful of the circumstances of the attack. The day after Pearl Harbor, the United States, powerfully united and vowing vengeance, declared war on Japan. 'Avenge December 7' was to be a powerful slogan in subsequent wartime propaganda posters (see front cover). Adolf Hitler declared war on America a few days after the Japanese attack. For more than two years there had been impassioned debate in America about whether and how the United States should respond to Japanese and German territorial expansion and support countries which were under attack. Almost overnight there was a collective realisation that the United States was part of a world community, with which its destiny was inextricably interlinked. In a transatlantic telephone call to Winston Churchill, the British Prime Minister, soon after the attack President Roosevelt commented, we are all in the same boat now.

Churchill recognised the Pearl Harbor attack as a turning point in the Second World War. Although conscious of short-term allied losses, he was more impressed by the long term implications of the attack. 'To have the United States at our side', he later wrote, 'was to me the greatest joy ... Now at this very moment I knew the United States was in the war, up to the neck and in to the death. So we had won after all!' The Pearl Harbor attack also represented a significant turning point in American foreign policy. The basis of United States neutrality before Pearl Harbor was isolationism, a policy advocating non-involvement in the affairs of other nations. A leading isolationist politician, Senator Vandenberg, noted in his memoirs, 'In my own mind, my convictions regarding international co-operation and collective security for peace took firm hold on the afternoon of the Pearl Harbor attack. That day ended isolationism for any realist.'

Isolationism helped to keep America out of the First World War until April 1917, contributed to the rejection by the United States Senate of membership of the League of Nations after the First World War, and was strong during the Republican party administrations of the 1920s. In the face of economic depression at home and international instability overseas, isolationist sentiment peaked in the mid-1930s. Opinion polls in 1939 still showed that a staggering 99 per cent of American people opposed American involvement in a foreign war. Although this figure was to change through 1940 and 1941, in the light of Nazi and Japanese annexations of territory, only the Japanese attack on Pearl Harbor finally undermined isolationist sentiment and it did so instantly and completely. American entry into the Second World War heralded a fundamental political, economic, and social transformation and the United States would emerge from the war not exhausted and traumatised like the other combatants but as the most powerful nation in the world. The Second World War produced a profound shift in the broad popular and expert consensus about foreign policy in the United States from 'isolationism' to 'internationalism'. In other words, America was prepared by 1945 to assume global leadership and responsibilities.

There were many dramatic twists and turns in the conduct of America's foreign relations between 1917 and 1945 and beyond. Not all roads necessarily led to Pearl Harbor and a place for the United States on the international stage. There had been similarly lively and divisive debates within American governing circles between 1914 and 1917 as were to be played out 25 years later concerning the benefits and limitations of American neutrality as a response to bloody conflict in Europe. In April 1917, as in December 1941, America eventually advanced to the rescue of the 'Old World' in the face of militaristic challenges that threatened civilised and democratic values and the United States' national interests. A number of major events occurred in the period covered by this book - including American entry into the First World War in 1917, peacemaking at the Versailles conference in 1919 and the subsequent rejection by the American Senate of membership of the League of Nations, German and Japanese territorial expansion in the 1930s, Pearl Harbor, the Yalta and Potsdam conferences of 1945, and the dropping of the atomic bombs on Hiroshima and Nagasaki in 1945.

Historians have disagreed in their interpretations of why most of these events occurred as they did and what were their main consequences. This means that there are no interpretations that are generally accepted as being 'right'. It will therefore be for you as you read this book to reach conclusions of your own on the major issues discussed and to be prepared to support these with reasoned arguments. Sometimes, no doubt, this will involve disagreeing with what you read in the following chapters.

2 The USA Assumes a Global Role

In the period between 1917 and 1945, the years separating American entry into the First World War and the end of the Second World War, the United States emerged as the most important global power. Significantly, this occurred despite the supposed isolation of the country from international political affairs in the 1920s and 1930s. This book will seek to make sense of how and why the United States achieved its pre-eminence. It would be easy to conclude, bearing in mind the size of America's population, its vast natural resources, and its industrial might, that there was a virtual inevitability about America's rise to superpower status by the mid-twentieth century. For much of the nineteenth century, America and Russia had been spoken of in the same breath by influential thinkers as the two powers whose vast size and population guaranteed them eventual supremacy. However, by the early twentieth century America's promise seemed the greater. The American Civil War in the 1860s had removed the possibility that the Union would disintegrate, the process of continental expansion to the American west coast was complete, and rapid industrialisation had closed the gap between the American economy and those of Britain, the dominant industrial power, and Germany. In 1913 the United States produced one-third of the world's manufactures, its coal output equalled that of Britain and Germany combined, and its iron and steel production was more than that of the whole continent of Europe. The trend seemed clear; America had the strength and wealth to dominate the world. But although the underlying facts of geography and economics undoubtedly do much to explain why America rose, they tell us less about the timing and form of its emergence as a superpower. In many ways America was relatively slow to assume global pre-eminence given its industrial strength by the start of the First World War. Indeed, many of the American people were reluctant to see their country become involved in the harsh realities of international relations. They wanted to see the United States stay clear of the political intrigues of Europe and Asia. We shall see that such attitudes were an important influence on American governments and leaders as they sought to promote and protect American interests in this period.

From the early years of the twentieth century American policy-makers appreciated the potential power of the United States in the world but there were limits to the way that America sought to project her power. In 1914 America was still a largely regional power in the Western hemisphere (in other words North, Central, and South America and the Caribbean), with tiny armed forces, which showed little desire to become involved in European conflicts. The Monroe Doctrine, formulated by President James Monroe and his Secretary of State John Quincy Adams in 1823, carried a great deal of weight in debates about America's relationship with the rest of the world. This called for a 'hands-off' policy by the European powers in the Western hemisphere (in other words, no new European colonies or dominions should be established in any part of the Americas), promised that the United States would stay out of 'Old World' quarrels because its democratic system differed from the monarchies of Europe, and denied American ambitions to colonize other countries.

Nevertheless, there had been considerable territorial expansion between the 1880s and 1914. With the annexation of Puerto Rico, the establishment of a protectorate over Cuba, and the seizure of Panama, almost complete control was established over the Caribbean and the approaches to the strategically important Panama Canal. In addition, support was provided for pro-American factions in Central American countries such as Mexico, El Salvador, Honduras, and Nicaragua, and America regularly applied what President Theodore Roosevelt described as the 'big stick'. The occupation of Hawaii, Samoa, Guam, and the Phillipines (the latter two following the short-lived Spanish-American War of 1898) extended the American frontier to the western Pacific. Mediation in the Russo-Japanese War of 1905 further increased American influence in the affairs of East Asia. The building of a modern navy, influenced by the ideas of Captain Alfred Thayer Mahan, reflected and intensified expansionist tendencies. Mahan regarded sea power as the basis of national power. He warned that the United States should not allow a single foreign coaling station (used to refuel ships), within 3,000 miles of San Francisco on the American west coast.

By 1945 the American economy was even stronger compared with the other great powers. At the end of the Second World War, America, with 7 per cent of the world's population, accounted for 50 per cent of the world's manufacturing production, including 80 per cent of the world's cars. Explanations of America's 'rise to globalism' by 1945 need to be extended beyond a repetition of the country's natural and demographic advantages. It is significant, for example, that the growth of American power in the world coincided with the decline of European power. The world on the eve of the First World War was dominated by the Western European powers. Two world wars accelerated the increase in American industrial production. The European countries, preoccupied with the wars, lost many markets which were not regained. In terms of world manufacturing production, the combined share of Britain, Germany, France, and Belgium fell from 37.5 per cent to 29.5 per cent between 1913 and 1928 (the peak year of economic recovery). European countries also suffered enormous losses as a result of the wars in terms of population, damage to infrastructure, and the sheer cost of financing their operations. American money rescued the European economies at the end of both the World Wars. Britain's 'special relationship' with America was one of economic dependence as well as political co-operation, and this was true not only of Britain but also of the whole of Western Europe. America offered a political and economic lead at the end of the Second World War which contrasted with her earlier rejection of membership of the League of Nations at the end of the First World War. The USA became a charter member of the new United Nations in 1945 and the largest contributor to the support of its operations. Indeed, the United Nations took up permanent residence in New York City. The Second World War changed congressional attitudes; the Senate approved the UN Charter by a vote of 89-2. In economic affairs, America sponsored the Bretton Woods Conference of 1944 which established the International Monetary Fund for stabilising world currencies and the World Bank for lending money to emerging countries, both of which had their headquarters in Washington DC.

There have been a variety of explanations for the expansion of American global influence between 1917 and 1945. According to one influential school of American historians there was a coherence to American expansion which was motivated by a drive to conquer the economic markets of the world. In 1959 William Appleman Williams wrote an influential book entitled *The Tragedy of American Diplomacy* which advanced this thesis, and later historians extended his ideas. He placed much emphasis on the China-oriented 'Open Door' Notes published by Secretary of State John Hay in 1899 and 1900 which sought to 'safeguard for the world the principle of equal and impartial trade', and claimed that the declarations implied a determination to open the door for American trade and capital around the world. He argued that right up to the mid-twentieth century and beyond American policy-makers used the state's political, military, and financial resources to exert their country's influence abroad so as to capture markets, undermine the existing pre-eminence of established imperial powers like Britain, and facilitate the export of surplus American production. Williams' interpretation is important and needs to be understood because he applied it to most of the key events in American foreign relations between 1917 and 1945. For example, he argued that economic factors explained America's entry into the First World War and negotiating the peace. Making the world 'safe for democracy' in Wilson's terms, Williams argued, meant creating a liberal capitalist system. According to Williams, such thinking also lay behind the Versailles peace settlement which was designed to safeguard Europe from the threat of a communist Russia and its alternative economic system.

Although it is important to recognise American economic interests in seeking international trade and furthering her global economic influence, other historians have disputed Williams' 'Open Door' explanation of American expansion. For example, it has been shown that foreign markets had a low priority in the American business consciousness. Woodrow Wilson wrote in 1919, 'It is amazing to me ... that the businessmen of America have concerned themselves so little with the commerce of the world, as distinguished from the commerce of

America.' The American home market was the destination for the overwhelming majority of American manufactured products in this period. By 1932, because of economic depression and world-wide protection, exports had fallen to 2.8 per cent of the Gross National Product. There are also other reasons for doubting the validity of Williams' thesis. Among these are the 'Open Door' school of historians' tendency to see the world beyond America as passive and powerless, its destiny determined by decisions made in Washington. They also tend to ignore the fact that there was a range of strategic, ideological, and prestige reasons which lay behind American expansion. American interest in China, for example, was as much about international prestige as economics. Moreover, it is difficult to demonstrate that economic factors were at the forefront of the minds of either Woodrow Wilson or Franklin Delano Roosevelt as they committed America to involvement in European and global conflicts. Rather, both feared the increasing power of Germany as an international menace, realised that it was not in the interests of the United States to see Europe dominated by a single power, and had a sincere wish to uphold American political and social values.

In addition to economic explanations for the expansion of American influence, a variety of other explanations have been suggested. These have included extending the idea that America had a 'Manifest Destiny' to conquer and civilise inferior peoples (a theory which had been used in explanations of the westward continental expansion of the United States in the nineteenth century). Certainly American leaders often sought to justify American expansion in idealistic terms. There were many missionary and moralistic flourishes to American diplomacy. They were evident in Wilson's Fourteen Points announced in January 1918, the principles of international conduct embodied in the Washington Treaties of 1921 (see page 106), countless statements of principle by Cordell Hull, the Secretary of State, in the 1930s, and the Atlantic Charter which included President Roosevelt's 'Four Freedoms' (see page 130). Throughout the period 1917 to 1945 America sought to apply to the world a body of general principles of conduct. There was a self-confident assumption that America was the anointed guardian of international behaviour, laying down the moral law to other less principled countries. There was some cynicism overseas about American claims to moral disinterestedness. Woodrow Wilson and Franklin Delano Roosevelt were supreme exponents of marrying national interests to idealistic hope but when it came to the crunch the national interest came first.

Other historians have seen American expansion as part of a continuing quest for physical security and have interpreted the actions of politicians and military men as seeking to extend national power. Analysing the conflicting concepts of idealism and realism (sometimes described as pragmatism) has been a major theme for historians of

American foreign relations in this period. When American leaders talked in abstract terms about the defence of freedom and liberty there were clearly limits to the extent they were willing or able to support their rhetoric with action. For example, reading the diaries and private papers of President Truman and his top advisers as the Cold War began to develop in 1945, some historians have been surprised how little attention they initially paid to moral factors, such as the human costs of Stalin's ruthless economic and social policies in the Soviet Union. What went on in Russia, the President noted to his wife, was Russia's business. The Soviet people had no democracy, but 'they evidently like their government or they wouldn't die for it'. There had been a similar silence in the face of Nazi abuses in the 1930s. American policy-makers did not speak out in defence of or give refuge to the millions of persecuted Jews (there was only a small relaxation of immigration quotas in 1938). Moreover, there was to be little or no moral debate over the rights and wrongs of dropping atomic bombs on Japanese cities in August 1945 (see page 144). Like all nations, the United States usually acted out of self-interest but Americans always thought that they could reconcile their ideals with their own national interest. It is clear that the problem of reconciling national self-interest with universal ideals transcending the interests of particular nations forms a central theme of any analysis of America's foreign relations in the first half of the twentieth century. Historians continue to debate vigorously how and why America exercised and extended her power abroad.

3 The Making of American Foreign Policy

Who has been in charge of American foreign policy? At the top, of course, was the President. Woodrow Wilson, Herbert Hoover, and Franklin Delano Roosevelt were all individuals who thought deeply about foreign affairs. This book pays considerable attention to the thinking and actions of Wilson and Roosevelt in particular - America's leaders during the two world wars. Such an approach is justifiable in view of the ways that these two enormously influential and charismatic men operated. Most studies of Woodrow Wilson, particularly outside America, have concentrated on the last phases of his career: the peacemaking at Paris and his failure to gain acceptance in America of the League of Nations covenant. Did he compromise too much with his principles where the peace was concerned and yet show himself too rigid in the face of his domestic critics? These questions are considered in detail in Chapter 3. For Wilson to play the role that he did at Paris, the United States had to be among the victor powers - yet American participation in the First World War seemed for a long time almost out of the question, both because of the immense popular reluctance to get involved, and because of Wilson's own views on his country's proper role. Although by 1917 there were important American interests supporting the Allied side, it is clear that these in themselves would have been insufficient to propel an unwilling nation into battle. The movement of Wilson's own mind was in many ways the decisive element not only in the decision for America to enter the war but also in its timing, and above all in the way in which the case for American entry was presented to the American nation and to the world. These issues are explored in Chapter 2.

Roosevelt, too, dominated the making of foreign policy during his entire administration and much recent historical work on the period 1933-45 has concentrated on the President's thoughts, personality, and actions. For example, an appreciation of Roosevelt's attitude to the worsening international situation in the 1930s and how the United States should respond to it, or to the future of US-Soviet relations towards the end of the Second World War, is fundamental in reaching an understanding of American policy on these issues. Historians have long debated the relative weight that should be given to idealistic and pragmatic motives in Roosevelt's foreign policies. Unsurprisingly, no consensus has emerged. It was difficult to disentangle Roosevelt's motives when he was alive, and the task has not become any easier since his death. For example, there were tensions between the Atlantic Charter (the statement of principles agreed by America and Britain at the beginning of the Second World War) and the horse-trading of territory and commitments at the Yalta Conference in February 1945 (see Chapter 6). Could the President have done more to counter German, Italian, and Japanese aggression in the 1930s? Might he have made greater efforts to counter the strength of domestic isolationism? When you read Chapters 4, 5 & 6 you will have an opportunity to decide for yourself where Roosevelt should be placed on the spectrum between idealism and realism. Many of Roosevelt's idealistic public statements were delivered to keep elements within his domestic audience happy but were contradicted by his pragmatic private comments and actions.

As you work to build up an understanding of the Presidents' decisions you will need to be aware of the range of advice available to them. It is important to know the sometimes tiny circle whose members, as in any other court, possessed influence through the right of access. The principal adviser entrusted with foreign affairs was the Secretary of State. Sometimes the Secretary of State could be a key policy-maker - Charles Evans Hughes (1921-5) comes into this category - but equally he could largely be sidelined by a strong President: Robert Lansing (1915-19) and Cordell Hull (1933-44) suffered innumerable snubs and were rarely able to influence the direction of policy. Military leaders, Treasury Secretaries, ambassadors, and more junior state department officials also had influence on occasions. Moreover, sometimes the President's personal staff achieved positions of dominance in the conduct of foreign policy. Colonel Edward M. House and Harry Hopkins both for a time reached positions of considerable trust and influence with Presidents Wilson and Roosevelt respectively before falling from favour.

Congressional opinion was another significant element in the making of American foreign policy. The divide in the American constitution between the executive and legislative branches of government complicated policy making. All twentieth century presidents have wanted to use Congress to ratify their foreign policies but none has wanted to share power with the lawmakers. Members of Congress did not always passively accept their role as meek supporters of the President's proposals. For example, although Congress supported the decision for war overwhelmingly in 1917, Wilson fell out with Congress spectacularly from 1918. There is a case for arguing that by his call for a Democratic Congress in 1918, by his failure to include a prominent Republican or Senator in the American peace delegation, and by his vow that 'the Senate must take its medicine', Woodrow Wilson unnecessarily politicised peace-making after the First World War and, in effect, kept the United States from joining the League of Nations (see pages 54-63). Usually the interests of representatives differed from those of the executive because Congressmen bowed to their constituents' wishes whilst the job of the President and State Department was to look to the wider international effects of measures. In the 1920s, for example, much as Republican officials yearned for export markets abroad, Congress was unwilling to give up the protection of the home market and kept tariffs high. Trading partners therefore raised their tariffs on imports making it harder for American companies to sell their goods abroad. Much as the same officials wanted international financial stability, Congress was reluctant to cancel war debts or to raise taxes, both of which contributed to continuing global financial instability. Sometimes the foreign policy benefits of policies did not outweigh the domestic costs as far as Congress was concerned.

Congressional influence reached its height in the mid-1930s. With war clouds looming over Europe and Asia, and with little initial opposition from the White House, Congress passed Neutrality Acts in 1935, 1936, and 1937 (see page 75). These were a series of laws that aimed to keep the United States out of overseas wars. Later in the 1930s and into the early 1940s Roosevelt found various ways of avoiding congressional opposition. Relying on international events and his own finely-honed political skills, he waited for the right moment to allow congressional debate on such measures as conscription and Lend-Lease, both of which eventually passed with large majorities. More often, Roosevelt expanded presidential powers and avoided consulting Congress, as when he obtained overseas allies and bases and waged undeclared economic and naval war against the axis powers. The subordination of Congress continued during and after the Second World War.

Public opinion and the press could also not be ignored by American

Presidents who had to renew their mandate with the electorate every four years. Roosevelt strove constantly not to repeat Wilson's errors in 1918-19, or his own decision to support American membership of the League of Nations in 1920, which had ignored both public opinion and the domestic political context in which decisions were made. In the 1920s America quietly re-entered the international system, took an active part in the world disarmament conference, and underwrote much of the Franco-German settlement on reparations. Although public opinion, both in Congress and the country, was a long way behind such moves, it was inching steadily towards a policy of intervention under pressure from the peace and disarmament lobbies. Therefore it would be a mistake to see American public opinion as being uniformly isolationist. Nevertheless, by the 1930s, as the effects of the Great Depression made themselves felt, Roosevelt's foreign policy was constrained by the isolationist sentiments of the majority of American voters. A desire among many Americans to withdraw in disgust from the world's woes led to widespread support for the neutrality laws of the 1930s. Later came the establishment of the America First Committee which campaigned against American entry into the Second World War. Of course, Presidents could attempt to lead as well as follow public opinion, and both Woodrow Wilson and Roosevelt demonstrated their skills in this respect. Nonetheless, little doubt exists that public opinion, as expressed through newspaper editorials, letters to the President, and, in the latter part of the period, opinion polls, counted for much in determining the course of American foreign relations between 1917 and 1945.

Business interests, too, had an important role in the making of American foreign policy. As described above (see page 5), some historians have argued that the interests of big business and corporations in seeking the expansion of foreign markets were the dominant force behind policy-making. American banks, industries, export associations, organised labour, and farm groups all represented powerful lobbies which pushed for market-oriented, Open Door strategies that served the interests of corporate America. As US officials and public opinion rejected a global political role for America in the 1920s, there is a good case for arguing that business interests had a powerful influence on policy. The economic power of the United States was directed towards Latin America, the Far East, and other regions of the world where the United States competed for economic advantage and markets at the expense of the older imperial powers such as Britain and France. Moreover, US loans to Europe, on which depended the cycle of German reparations to the Allies and allied debt payments to the United States did not originate from the US government but private banks. There is an absence of evidence proving that industrialists and financiers controlled specific decisions, but it has been argued that policy-makers had internalised 'Open Door' theories and the necessity of expansion.

President Calvin Coolidge commented in 1928, 'Our investments and trade relations are such that it is almost impossible to conceive of any conflict anywhere on earth which would not affect us injuriously.' The American government was never simply the puppet of special economic and business interests but was clearly influenced by them.

Finally, it is necessary to consider the impact of international events and external pressures on America's foreign relations. Many events were beyond the control of Washington policy-makers. For example, Woodrow Wilson had to respond to the launching of unrestricted German submarine warfare in early 1917 and the different peacemaking agendas of the other great powers at Paris in 1919. In the 1930s, in the face of a series of threatening and potentially dangerous events, the current posture of standing idly on the sidelines came to seem more and more questionable. By the time of Roosevelt's second Inaugural Speech in 1936 the decade had already seen the Japanese conquest of Manchuria, the rise of Hitler, the German remilitarisation of the Rhineland (forbidden under the terms of the Versailles treaty), the Italian invasion of Abyssinia, and the beginning of the Spanish Civil War. The President confessed to one correspondent in 1936 that, 'The whole European panorama is fundamentally blacker than at any time in your life ... or mine.' A year later it was said that 'the President's attitude is one of complete helplessness about the European situation'. As Roosevelt tentatively and loosely aligned America with Britain and France in Europe, and with China in Asia after 1938, his policies were largely reactions to the aggressive expansion of Nazi and Japanese militarism. Much of international relations in the early part of the Second World War from 1939-41 was unpredictable - not least Pearl Harbor. America's Pacific War against Japan from 1941 to 1945 was largely the result of Japan's failure to prevent its struggle with China from escalating into a wider struggle. Thus, to gain a full appreciation of American-Japanese relations in the 1930s and 1940s it is important to understand the Japanese and Chinese context and perspective as well as the American point of view (see Chapter 5).

In the face of an abundance of often conflicting advice, political and domestic concerns, and unpredictable external events, the making of American foreign policy was not easy. At several points in this book you will have an opportunity to put yourselves into the shoes of American leaders and assess their decisions with the advantage of hindsight. They did not have this luxury. Often decisions had to be taken rapidly and under pressure in less than ideal circumstances. Economic and military realities often reduced the available options. Why did Wilson hesitate to intervene in Europe between 1914 and 1916 but choose to do so in 1917? Should Wilson be praised or blamed for his handling of peacemaking between 1918 and 1920? How adamantly isolationist was the United States in the 1930s? Was a compromise settlement with Japan possible at any point between 1937 and 1941? Was the Yalta agreement of February 1945 a sell-out or the best possible deal in the circumstances? How justifiable was the decision of President Truman to drop atomic bombs on Hiroshima and Nagasaki in August 1945? There are no clear-cut and certain answers to these questions, some of which involve issues where the moral values of the person answering are all-important. In this book you will find a series of informed judgements which constitute the author's version of the most appropriate answers. It will be for you to decide which of these to accept, possibly with modifications, and which to reject.

Making notes on *'Introduction: The USA and the World 1917-45'*

There is no need to make notes on this chapter in the normal way, but it will be worth your while doing some work to make sure that you have understood and remembered the main points that have been made. One of the main aims of the chapter has been to help you create a mental map of the chronological shape of this period of American foreign affairs. To consolidate this (or it may just be a matter of checking that it has been done) look at the chronological table of events at the back of this book. Many of the events mentioned will be no more than names at the moment. This is nothing to be worried about - you will find out what you need to know about them as you read the rest of the book. Your task at this stage is to divide the years 1917 to 1945 into a number of periods each of which has some unifying factor. There is no way in which you should identify less than 3 and if you select more than 6 you are probably overlooking the factors which provide the genuine coherence to each period. Make a list of the periods you have chosen, and briefly explain what provides each with its unity.

Now look at the two summary diagrams. Write a brief sentence about each entry to show that you understand what it means and what its significance is.

Is there anything else in the chapter that you think it would be worth you remembering? If there is, make a note of it. Now you are ready to move on to Chapter 2.

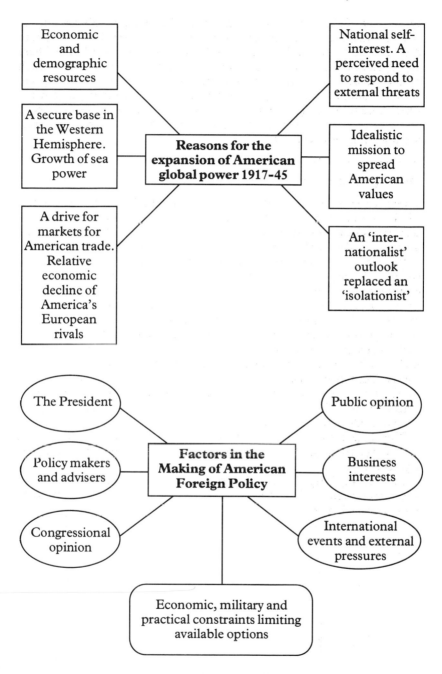

Economic and demographic resources

A secure base in the Western Hemisphere. Growth of sea power

A drive for markets for American trade. Relative economic decline of America's European rivals

Reasons for the expansion of American global power 1917-45

National self-interest. A perceived need to respond to external threats

Idealistic mission to spread American values

An 'inter-nationalist' outlook replaced an 'isolationist'

The President

Policy makers and advisers

Congressional opinion

Factors in the Making of American Foreign Policy

Public opinion

Business interests

International events and external pressures

Economic, military and practical constraints limiting available options

Summary - Introduction: The USA and the World, 1917-45

CHAPTER 2

The USA and the First World War

1 Introduction

In 1916 Woodrow Wilson spoke approvingly of the Farewell Address delivered in 1796 by America's first President, George Washington, 'You know that we have always remembered and revered the advice of the great Washington, who advised us to avoid foreign entanglements. By that I understand him to mean to avoid being entangled in the ambitions and the national purposes of other nations.' Yet less than a year later the Wilson administration rejected George Washington's warnings and committed American citizens to fight in Europe. President Wilson's decision to declare war on Germany in April 1917, endorsed overwhelmingly by votes in the Senate and the House of Representatives, marked a major turning point in America's foreign relations. The intervention of the United States in the First World War was to prove decisive to its outcome.

The initial response of Woodrow Wilson to the outbreak of hostilities in Europe in August 1914 had been to declare a firm position of American neutrality in keeping with America's traditional isolationism in foreign affairs. He urged Americans to be 'neutral in fact as well as name ... impartial in thought as well as action'. There were a few critics, for example Theodore Roosevelt, a former President, and a defeated Progressive candidate in the election of 1912, described the neutrality proclamation as 'cowardly and unworthy'. Nevertheless, Wilson's advisers and a great majority of the American people were in general agreement that a neutral stance was the best course for the United States. The country appeared to have no vital stake in the war and American national security was not immediately threatened. However, maintaining a balanced neutrality proved to be difficult, and it soon became apparent that the war did affect American interests. Wilson recognised this in his second inaugural speech in March 1917 - 'We are provincials no longer ... The tragical events of the thirty months of vital turmoil through which we have just passed have made us citizens of the world. There can be no turning back. Our own fortunes as a nation are involved, whether we would have it so or not.' He promoted the idea that the United States had an historic mission to bring Europe into a peaceful world order based on international law.

2 Public Opinion and Neutrality, 1914-17

Whilst not a prisoner of public opinion, Woodrow Wilson was keenly aware of the attitudes of the American people, stating as early as 1890 as a Princeton Lecturer in Political Science, that 'The ear of the leader must ring with the voices of the people.' The public opinion of a large and diverse nation during such a period of crisis cannot be measured with any great precision. Yet as measured by the statements of most governors, senators, and congressmen, and the majority of newspapers and periodicals, Wilson's foreign policy generally commanded support. Most Americans refused to believe that their country would be affected one way or the other by the outcome of a European war. Indeed, most Americans possessed only a limited understanding or interest in the world beyond their shores. The issues at stake seemed remote and puzzling. The long established tradition of abstention from Europe's politics and wars and the width of the Atlantic seemed to ensure that America would stay out. Neutrality would help to shelter American dreams of the progressive betterment of mankind from the complexities of traditional European power politics.

Both the Allies and the Central Powers recognised the importance of public opinion, and the American people were deluged with a flood of propaganda and appeals on behalf of the opposing alliances. The readership for German appeals included over eight million German-Americans who, judging by the attitudes of their newspapers and social organisations, were inclined to be strongly sympathetic to the German cause. Four million Irish Americans tended to favour the cause of the Central Powers, having imbibed centuries of bitterness at British government of Ireland. Moreover, practically all those who were immigrants from the Russian and Austro-Hungarian empires, from Lithuanian-Americans to Slovak-Americans and Hungarian-Americans, also tended to support the cause of Germany and Austria-Hungary. At the outbreak of the European war, President Wilson remarked, only partly tongue-in-cheek, 'We definitely have to be neutral since otherwise our mixed populations would wage war on each other.' At least early in the war, the propaganda campaigns probably evened out in terms of their effectiveness. Some of the details of the German propaganda machine were revealed and consequently discredited when US secret agents picked up a briefcase left by a New York-based secret agent on a train and its contents were published in leading newspapers.

Nevertheless, if the majority of Americans were probably mildly pro-allied from autumn 1914 onwards, there were times during the war when Anglo-American relations were remarkably poor - notably the summer of 1916. The British blockaded all neutral commerce to Germany in an attempt to strangle the German economy, and this was seen as an extension of Britain's sea dominion and a disruption of the 'freedom of the seas'. The blockade imposed significant restrictions on US commerce; American trade with the Central Powers was largely halted. In addition, American opinion was outraged at the brutal suppression by the British authorities of the Easter Rising in Ireland in April 1916 and the subsequent trial and execution of its leaders. At the same time, the seizure and examination of parcels in American mail en route to Europe and the blacklisting by the British government of 437 American and Latin American firms with whom British subjects were forbidden to deal because they were thought to be working in Germany's interests, created a large amount of bad feeling. For a short time Wilson came to see British 'navalism' as on a par with German 'militarism'.

However, effective allied propaganda probably had some effect in strengthening the pro-ally sentiments held by most Americans. As a result, the entry of the United States into the war on the side of Germany was unthinkable, while entry on the side of the Allies was not inconceivable. American attitudes were conditioned by the background of German-American rivalries in the Far East, a fear that Germany had naval ambitions in the Caribbean, and a deep-rooted distrust of the Kaiser and the military elite that controlled Germany. Germany had refused to submit the Serbian question to arbitration and had broken treaty pledges in violating Belgian neutrality. British propaganda made good use of alleged German atrocities in Northern France and Belgium, the deportation of some 300,000 Belgians for forced labour in the Reich, the German army's use of poison gas, and incidents such as the execution of Nurse Edith Cavell as a spy in 1915. Above all, the severity of allied economic warfare was eclipsed in the eyes of most Americans by the German government's novel method of retribution - submarine warfare.

The use of submarine warfare was first announced by Germany in February 1915. German submarines would sink without warning enemy merchant vessels in a war zone around Britain. Neutral vessels were advised to stay out of the zone to avoid accidents. America was the wealthiest neutral state and the most important neutral carrier. The German justification for her move was that it was impossible for submarines to give conventional notice of their intention to sink a merchant ship without endangering themselves. Nor was it possible to make adequate provision for the safety of passengers. In the light of this unprecedented action, Wilson drafted a note to Germany declaring that the United States would hold the German government to a 'strict accountability' for damages to Americans which might result from the new policy. Yet on 7 May 1915 a German submarine torpedoed the British liner *Lusitania,* with the subsequent death of almost 1200 civilians, including 128 Americans. The news created such an impact in the United States that 10 years later a writer found that everyone he interviewed still vividly remembered where they had been, and what they had thought and felt, when they first heard the news. The war was no longer 'over there'. But almost no-one called for war. In a poll of newspaper editors throughout the country, only six out of 1,000 said that America should fight Germany. The overwhelming sentiment was still decidedly non-interventionist.

Wilson's response was a demand that the German government 'take immediate steps to prevent the recurrence of anything so obviously subversive of the principles of warfare'. A repetition of the sinkings would be regarded as 'deliberately unfriendly'. Wilson was reluctant to break diplomatic relations with Germany, despite the opportunity offered by continued sinkings, because by doing so he would lose his leverage as a diplomatic mediator. In August 1915, the German Emperor was persuaded to order the abandonment of unrestricted warfare against all passenger ships following the sinking of the British liner *Arabic*. When the channel steamer *Sussex* was torpedoed on 24 March 1916, injuring four Americans, Wilson and Secretary of State Lansing finally informed the German government that unless they gave up submarine warfare, the United States would break off diplomatic relations. The German response was the 'Sussex pledge' of 3 May, conceding to the American demand. After the Spring of 1916 the U-boat campaign was suspended because German leaders saw no point in alienating the Americans whilst the submarines were not yet in a position to deliver a knockout blow to the British. Having achieved a diplomatic victory, as long as Germany paid at least lip service to her pledge, Wilson would pursue his neutral course relentlessly. During 1915 and 1916 he was aware that he could not have hoped to carry a united country with him to war - if indeed he could have extracted a declaration of war out of Congress. The great majority of Americans did not want war and the President shared their sentiments, remarking in 1915: 'Our whole duty for the present, at any rate, is summed up by this motto: America first.' In Spring 1916 a Senate resolution called upon the State Department to warn Americans against travelling on any armed ship, thereby hoping to avoid any future flashpoint. If the President had been thinking of abandoning neutrality, obviously many Americans, especially in his own party, were not. There was powerful support for continued neutrality from the delegates at the Democratic National Convention at St. Louis in June 1916. At the 1916 election, an increase of almost three million in his popular vote since 1912 was a measure of the extent to which Wilson had won the confidence of the American people.

The President had to walk a diplomatic and domestic tightrope (see the illustration) and undertake an uncomfortable balancing act between neutrality and internationalism, fear of involvement in the hostilities, and a great desire to help bring them to a close. In private conversations and correspondence his broad sympathies with Britain were clear but he articulated a carefully balanced attitude in public. At home, progressive opponents of involvement in the war were suspicious of the 'preparedness' campaign to which Wilson committed himself publicly in autumn 1915. William Bryan, his former Secretary of State, remarked: 'The nation does not need burglars' tools unless it intends to make burglary its business.' Nevertheless, uncertain of his ability to maintain the balance, Wilson spent much of 1916 preparing the American people

for war, while stressing to the belligerents that he was in favour of peace.
A National Defence Act of June 1916 enlarged the regular army to
220,000 and integrated the National Guard into a defence system whilst
a Naval Appropriation Bill in August 1916 authorised the construction
of a large number of new battleships and cruisers.

The policy of neutrality itself was also a perpetual balancing act,
although here the balance tipped consistently in favour of the allied side.
For example, neutrality policies as regards the munitions trade, credits
and loans, and acquiescence in the British blockade of the Central
powers operated strongly in favour of the Allies. Wilson's dealings with
Britain differed in two significant respects from his problems with
Germany. First, British violations of neutrality did not result in the
deaths of Americans, but Germany's actions did, particularly its reliance

A cartoon from the Chicago Tribune, *summer 1915*

on the submarine. Thus, the disputes with Britain would be able to be resolved at the end of the war because they involved only money and property, but it would be too late to settle those with Germany. As Senator Henry Cabot Lodge, often a leading critic of Wilson, put it, he was more moved by the spectacle of women and children drowning in the ocean than by that of American cotton sitting on a wharf. Second, the British played the American game much better than Germany did. Ties of language and literature, law and custom bound America (and Wilson himself) to Britain. The domestic constraints under which Wilson operated were sympathetically and astutely relayed to London by the British ambassador, Sir Cecil Spring Rice and, as a result, the frictions were managed effectively. As part of a general strategy to court American goodwill, Britain encouraged Wilson to believe that, at some indefinite point in the future, he would be allowed to help end the war.

Having noted the imbalance in the implementation of specific neutrality policies, it is important to underline that the Wilson administration was sincere about neutrality. It was a way to occupy the moral high ground and show the world how to live in peace. The example of the United States would be the example of the just and good. Following the sinking of the *Lusitania*, Wilson proclaimed that: 'There is such a thing as a man being too proud to fight. There is such a thing as a nation being so right that it does not need to convince others by force that it is right.' There were some mutterings of discontent at this statement but Wilson meant only that America 'must be a special example' because it obeyed the law. Through its actions, the United States would show that 'peace is the healing and elevating influence of the world and [that] strife is not'. The role of the United States was 'to preserve the foundations upon which peace can be rebuilt'. Wilson insisted on the rights of neutrality because his vision of the future depended upon respect for international law.

3 The Decision for War

Wilson's response to the war alternated between a desire to intervene constructively in order to shape international events and a conviction that America should maintain a strict neutrality. On the one hand, the President hoped to act as an impartial mediator and help to end the fighting in Europe. He launched a number of initiatives to break the military stalemate and achieve a 'peace without victory'. On the other hand, a firm wish to keep his nation out of the conflict underpinned Wilson's policies towards both the Allies and the Central Powers until as late as March 1917. The policies were not incompatible but the American people certainly showed no wish to become involved in the European conflict. In 1916 Wilson won a close-fought presidential election with the popular campaign slogan 'He Kept Us Out Of The War'. In January 1917 he was to tell Edward House, his foreign affairs adviser and confidant, 'There will be no war. This country does not intend to become involved in this war ... it would be a crime against civilisation for us to go in.' Only three months later, however, Wilson requested Congress to declare that a state of war existed between Germany and the United States. The President who, according to his Attorney General, 'hated war more than any man I ever knew' was forced into the decision by policy makers in Berlin.

On 31 January 1917 the German Ambassador, Bernstorff, delivered a note to the State Department announcing that Germany would henceforth engage in unrestricted submarine warfare which would spare no ships, including those of neutrals. The decision was made in the certain knowledge that it would inevitably bring America into the war. Bernstorff noted in his diary, 'The people in Berlin knew what was bound to happen if they took the action they have taken. There was nothing else left for the United States to do.' The German military high command decided to gamble upon all-out victory, believing that they could starve Britain into submission before the United States could have a significant military impact upon the European theatre of war (Germany's domestic situation was increasingly desperate by this stage as the British naval blockade proved cumulatively effective). Despite the fact that Germany was now committed to destroy US shipping and to sink ships carrying US citizens, the German note did not trigger an immediate declaration of war. For Wilson only the actual commitment of these 'overt acts' could bring hostilities. He went no further than breaking off diplomatic relations. Both House and Secretary of State Lansing urged Wilson to join the fight but the President told the latter that he was willing to go to almost any lengths 'rather than to have this nation actually involved in the conflict'. Instead, Wilson opted for a policy of armed neutrality, requesting authority from Congress on 26 February to arm American merchant ships. Even this decision was reached by Wilson with considerable reluctance.

An event that confirmed the aggressive intentions of the Imperial German government towards the United States was the interception and publication of the Zimmerman Telegram in February 1917. The telegram was from the German Foreign Minister, Arthur Zimmerman, to the German Minister in Mexico City, and proposed that, in the event of war between Germany and the United States, Mexico should enter the war on the side of Germany, receiving in return the territories of Texas, New Mexico, and Arizona lost in the Mexican War of 1846-8. Moreover, Japan should be invited to join the coalition against America. The effect of the telegram on American public opinion was to convince a previously neutral majority of the hostile intentions of the German government and to impel a reluctant nation closer to war. No matter how far-fetched the threat of Mexican involvement was, it brought the war closer to home. Lansing commented that the telegram 'in one day accomplished a change in sentiment and public opinion that otherwise would have required months to accomplish'. *The Omaha World Herald* stated that, 'The issue shifts from Germany against Great Britain to Germany against the United States.'

The direct threat to American territory both transformed the apathy of Western states and undermined opposition in German-American communities to Wilson's policies towards Berlin. As Senator Thomas of Colorado put it, 'The public mind has been inflamed by this publication like a bolt.' Ray Stannard Baker, Wilson's authorised biographer, contended that 'no single more devastating blow was delivered against Wilson's resistance to entering war' than the Zimmerman Telegram. Although there was no widespread enthusiasm for war, most citizens seemed to agree that American rights were in jeopardy and that their defence was more important than peace. A survey of 68 newspapers showed that only one opposed intervention after the war was declared. Nevertheless, whilst Wilson viewed the Telegram as a 'challenge of hostile purpose', it was not regarded as an 'overt act' necessitating a declaration of war. In a Presidential address on 5 March 1917 Wilson declared 'We stand firm in armed neutrality.'

This policy was ended by the sinkings, without warning and with heavy loss of life, of three American merchant vessels on 18 March by German U-boats. Whilst Wilson was still reluctant to declare war, the renewal of submarine attacks finally convinced the President that Germany was no longer interested in a negotiated end to the war and that German militarism was the main obstacle to peace. It was also at this time that an ideological obstacle to intervention was removed with the success of the first Russian Revolution. Whilst this did not directly influence the decision for war, the replacement of autocracy in Russia by a Provisional Government committed to constitutional reforms was interpreted by Wilson as evidence of the rise of democracy in the world. It thus furthered the cause of the Allies in the minds of the President and many American citizens. On 20 March the President called a meeting of his Cabinet, asking each member individually for his recommendation. The 10 councillors unanimously recommended war. Lansing argued that, 'The time for delay and inaction has passed . . . We are at war now. Why not say so without faltering? Silence will be interpreted abroad as weakness, at home as indecision.' As Wilson was preparing his 2 April Speech to Congress, Joseph Tumulty, his personal secretary examined the editorial opinion of the country's leading newspapers and concluded that: 'The consensus seems to be that the end of the war will be accomplished sooner if we go resolutely about it, in dead earnest, using all the energy we can immediately put forth in preparing ourselves simply to put all of our force into the struggle.'

In his speech to Congress on 2 April 1917 Wilson spoke clearly about the reasons why he felt war against Germany was now the only honourable alternative for a proud nation:

1 There is one choice we cannot make, we are incapable of making:
we will not choose the path of submission and suffer the sacred
rights of our nation and our people to be ignored or violated ... I
advise that Congress declare the recent course of the Imperial
5 German Government to be in fact nothing less than war against the
government and people of the United States; that it formally
accept the status of belligerent which has been thrust upon it.

The President also went beyond specific grievances, couching the war
decision in broader, ideological terms. The United States was going to
fight Germany, he said, because the latter had proved to be a menace to
world peace and civilisation. So long as German militarism remained,
there could be no secure peace:

1 Our object ... is to vindicate the principles of peace and justice in
the life of the world as against selfish and autocratic power and to
set up amongst the really free and self-governing peoples of the
world such a concert of purpose and of action as will henceforth
5 ensure the observance of those principles. Neutrality is no longer
feasible or desirable where the peace of the world is involved and
the freedoms of the peoples ...

America would now make its military power available to help determine
the outcome of the European conflict and, most important, to ensure
that the world would be 'made safe for democracy'. Wilson had long
been a committed internationalist and idealist in the realm of foreign
affairs, and he was therefore able to fit his decision into the wider context
of his principles. One of his major concerns from 1914 onwards was the
terms of the peace settlement whenever the conflict might end. By April
1917 events had pushed him to the conclusion that only as a participant
in war could the United States help to shape the subsequent peace.

There were a few critics of the decision for war. For example, Robert
La Follette, the Republican Senator for Wisconsin, disagreed that the
war was necessarily one for democracy:

1 The President proposes alliance with Great Britain, which,
however liberty-loving its people, is a hereditary monarchy, with a
hereditary ruler, with a hereditary House of Lords, with a
hereditary landed system ... The President has not suggested that
5 we make our support of Great Britain conditional to her granting
home rule to Ireland, or Egypt, or India. We rejoice in the
establishment of a democracy in Russia, but it will hardly be
contended that if Russia was still an autocratic government, we
would not be asked to enter this alliance with her just the same ...
10 Who has registered the knowledge or approval of the American
people of the course this Congress is called upon in declaring war

upon Germany? Submit the question to the people, you who support it. You who support it dare not do it, for you know that by a vote of more than ten to one the American people as a body 15 would register their declaration against it .

The final comment seems to have been an unsubstantiated exaggeration. Few of his colleagues agreed with La Follette. On 6 April Congress voted by 82-6 in the Senate and 373-50 in the House of Representatives to declare war on Germany.

Although there were good reasons for Wilson to take the United States into the war, there are still puzzling aspects of his decision. Wilson had been desperate to stay out of the war - 'if there is any alternative for God's sake let's take it' he exclaimed on 1 April 1917. It was unusual to uphold high-minded principles to the point of war. Other neutral nations such as Denmark and Norway lost more of their citizens from submarine attacks but did not go to war. Idealistic notions played a part in Wilson's thinking; in the President's view, 'We entered the war as the disinterested champions of right.' But democracy and 'a new international order based on the broad principles of right and justice' were war aims once the United States had entered the war rather than direct causes of America's entry into the war. By April 1917, however, there seemed to be no honourable alternative. The President had committed his country to uphold neutral rights. He had written that he 'would not consent to any abridgement of the rights of American citizens in any respect'. He refused to renounce responsibility for US citizens who travelled on belligerent ships. The President decided to make a stand over the question of neutral rights - a principle of international law which the German submarines were ignoring. On 2 April 1917, in his speech to Congress, Wilson accused Germany of 'throwing to the winds all scruples of humanity'. As he put it in the Summer of 1917, 'The military masters of Germany denied us the right to be neutral.'

4 The Foreign Policy Beliefs and Principles of Woodrow Wilson

Wilson brought firm ideas about the role of the President with him to the White House. In an academic study of constitutional government in the United States published in 1908 he wrote that, 'One of the greatest of the President's powers is control, which is very absolute, of the foreign relations of the nation.' As an academic he had several opportunities to speak and write about American foreign policy after 1898 and he formulated a coherent set of ideas which flowed from his religious faith and his convictions about political democracy. Most notably in his Fourteen Points, which were announced in a speech in January 1918, he espoused a new internationalist political ideology (see pages 41-2).

Ordered international relations and collective obligations would create a moral sense of world community. Wilson is often described as an idealist. Whilst this is accurate, it does not mean that he was incapable of common sense, practical appraisals, and political flexibility. It took an astute politician to achieve re-election in 1916 against the re-united Republicans who constituted the natural majority party. The fact that Wilson dominated Congress, which passed virtually everything he sent to them, also provides evidence that he was a shrewd political operator.

Wilson the diplomatist made all the final decisions himself. He routinely composed important diplomatic notes on his own typewriter and in many instances conducted diplomatic negotiations without informing the state department. He possessed a powerful intellect and a strong hold over both his party and the levers of foreign policy. He could appear arrogant, self-righteous, and deaf to advice. Many shared the later suspicion of the French premier, Georges Clemenceau, that Wilson thought himself a new messiah predestined to set the world right.

Yet the President did have key advisers. His most trusted counsellor was Edward M. House, a man of independent wealth, who for years was a major political power broker in Texas. Wilson once described him as 'my second personality ... his thoughts and mine are one'. Serving in an unofficial position, it was House who shuttled between the European capitals in January and February 1916 in search of peace between the Allies and the Central Powers. Out of the attempts at mediation grew the idea of a League of Nations. However, until his resignation in June 1915, no-one exerted a stronger influence on Wilson's foreign policy than his Secretary of State, William Jennings Bryan. Bryan was a veteran of three losing presidential campaigns and a much loved figure in the Democratic Party. He was the major link between the administration and the American peace movement, which was particularly strong in this period and championed arbitration and conciliation in foreign relations. Whilst somewhat naive and undiplomatic, his views were respected by Wilson. Bryan's successor, Robert Lansing, a lawyer and experienced state department official, was a less trusted and influential lieutenant than Bryan. Nevertheless, working in close co-operation with House, Lansing was able to achieve a measure of influence on Wilsonian foreign policy during the war years. They concluded earlier than the President that only an allied victory achieved with American support could secure the sort of peace the President wanted. Indeed, in mid-1915 Lansing confided in a private memorandum, 'Germany must not be permitted to win this war ... This ultimate necessity must be constantly in our minds ... American public opinion must be prepared for the time, which may come, when we will have to cast aside our neutrality and become one of the champions of democracy.'

American attempts at mediation in the First World War extended her role in world affairs and demonstrated her desire to make a constructive contribution in line with Wilsonian principles. They reflected a sense that the Europeans were incapable of managing their own affairs and that without some leadership role played by the United States there could be no stable international order. Nevertheless, one simple fact crippled Wilson's mediation diplomacy through the entire period of American neutrality; neither the Central Powers nor the Allies ever responded to him in an honest and open way. Both sides were dedicated to expansive war aims which required military victory and a dictated peace. Confident of success, German naval strategists, with the support of the Kaiser, held firm against any premature truce. For their part, Britain and France had reached secret agreements with Russia, Italy, and Japan to divide up the spoils of victory. They wanted the post-war territorial adjustments to reflect a victory at the expense of Germany and its allies. For example, Italy had been promised the restoration of territory in the Tyrol and on the Adriatic coast at the expense of the Austrian Empire. Each side made positive noises about a negotiated peace, general disarmament, and a new international organisation to ensure the post-war world order, but mainly did so in order not to upset Wilson unnecessarily. The American President saw imperialism, militarism, and the balance of power as the root causes of the European war and thus in his Peace Note of December 1916 suggested a universal system of collective security to replace the old alliances. The ultimate failure of American mediation efforts became clear when Germany announced the resumption of unrestricted submarine warfare in January 1917.

Involvement in the war prompted Wilson to set out his aspirations for a new world order. His vision has exerted great appeal for Americans and liberal thinkers ever since. Wilson's ideas were encapsulated in his Fourteen Points, which included calls for open diplomacy, freedom of the seas, removal of economic barriers among nations, reduction of armaments, the ending of imperialism, self-determination for national groups, and the creation of an association of nations to assume collective responsibility for maintaining the peace. A single thread ran through the programme - 'The principle of justice to all peoples and nationalities and the right to live on equal terms of liberty and safety with one another, whether they be weak or strong.' It can be seen as the culmination of a maturing ideological vision and it brought together a variety of ideas. Wilson skilfully synthesised the ideas of progressive internationalists inside and outside the United States whose ranks included feminists, liberals, pacifists, and socialists. He was influenced by the programmes of organisations such as the Woman's Peace Party, established in January 1915, and the American Union Against Militarism, created in April 1916. He also picked up many of the ideas of the Republican dominated League to Enforce Peace and, after a key speech to this group in May 1916 in which he endorsed the idea of collective security, virtually overnight secured for himself leadership of the American

League of Nations movement. In many of his speeches before January 1918, most notably in his address to the Senate in January 1917, Wilson had articulated a liberal peace programme - 'Victory would mean peace forced upon the loser ... It would be accepted in humiliation, under duress, at an intolerable sacrifice, and would leave a sting, a resentment, a bitter memory upon which terms of peace would rest, not permanently, but only as upon quicksand.'

Wilson had attempted to apply his ideas on a small scale in 1914-15 by proposing a Pan-American pact. His ambition was for the Western hemisphere 'to set an example to the world in freedom of institutions, freedom of trade, and intelligence of mutual service,' and to establish an exemplary structure of peace grounded in collective security. The proposal was eventually rejected by the Latin American countries. Partly this was as a result of an intervention by American troops in the Mexican Revolution of 1914-15. There had been a military coup led by Victoriano Huerta in 1911. Wilson feared that, if the Mexican leader remained in power, other Latin American revolutionaries would follow his example. Moreover, the United States had significant economic interests in Mexico, owning 43 percent of all property by value - 10 percent more than the Mexicans themselves owned. Wilson was determined to help other peoples become democratic and orderly and sought to stabilise and democratise the government of America's neighbour. Although Huerta was removed, following American pressure, in August 1914, his successor, Venustiano Carranza, proved just as hostile to American interests. Most notably, Carranza staked Mexico's claim to all its subsoil mineral rights and thus threatened United States oil companies. Wilson again sanctioned intervention in March 1916, which on this occasion failed to remove Carranza from power. In seeking to 'properly' direct the Mexican Revolution, Wilson twice invaded the country and killed Mexicans. Not surprisingly, America's actions smacked of heavy-handedness to Mexico's Latin American neighbours and made them suspicious of America's collective security proposals. Internal rivalries and suspicions between the individual Latin American states also helped to kill off the idea of a Pan American pact.

The Fourteen Points have been interpreted by many historians as America's response to the communist revolution in Russia. According to this view, Wilson was seeking to construct a peaceful liberal capitalist world order under international law, safe from both traditional imperialism and revolutionary socialism, within which America could spread progressive values and find moral and economic pre-eminence. Moreover, he was explicitly answering Lenin's calls for World Revolution and challenging the Bolshevik leader's belief in the inability of the international capitalist system to resolve its internal contradictions peacefully through rational reform. The sixth of the Fourteen Points demanded the evacuation of all Russian territory and the 'unembarrassed opportunity for the independent determination of her own political institutions'. Yet, apart from the one explicitly referring to Russia, none of the Fourteen Points was in any way inspired by the Bolsheviks. At this stage, Lenin was a fairly obscure politician at the head of a very shaky government about whom Wilson knew very little. The seven proposals for territorial adjustments would have been included in any circumstances. These were the evacuation of Belgium, the return of Alsace-Lorraine to France, the readjustment of Italian frontiers along recognisable lines of nationality, separate and independent development for the peoples of Austria-Hungary, the Balkans, and Turkey, and the creation of a Polish state with free and secure access to the sea. The remaining six were an integral part of Wilsonian principles before America entered the war and long before the revolutionary upheaval in Russia.

Wilson had several objectives in delivering his address in January 1918. Some of them were related to recent events in Russia. Ironically, Russian negotiators had recently agreed an armistice with Germany at Brest-Litovsk which included many Wilsonian principles, such as no forcible annexations, self-determination, no indemnities, and no economic boycotts or restrictions on freedom of trade. Two of Wilson's aims were to reduce the impact of the publication of the secret allied treaties recently published by the Russians and to try to bring the Bolsheviks back into the war against Germany through an appeal to common principles. He also hoped to stir up political discontent amongst opponents of the imperial regimes within Germany and Austria-Hungary by indicating the terms on which they could gain peace. Above all, however, Wilson sought to rally all groups at home and abroad behind a peace settlement grounded in a League of Nations and other new principles of international conduct, and to persuade the allied governments to embrace that cause, an aim he had been working to achieve since the Spring of 1916.

5 The American Economy and the First World War

The United States would have emerged as the leading economic power in the world even without the Great War but the European conflict accelerated the process. A combination of abundant natural resources, an almost inexhaustible supply of cheap labour resulting from immigration, and considerable capital investment had enormously stimulated the national economy in the early years of the twentieth century. By 1913 the United States had already become the largest economy in the world, producing over one third of its industrial output - just under the combined total of Germany, Britain, and France. With the demands of the war, European merchant ships virtually disappeared from Asia, the Middle East, and Latin America and American ships and traders were quick to fill the gap. By April 1917 America's total industrial potential and its share of world manufacturing output was two and a half times that of Germany's overstrained economy. It produced half the world's food exports which, after the declaration of war, could be sent to France and Italy as well as Britain. During the war there were also rapid increases in American investments and loans abroad. Virtually overnight the United States became the world's greatest creditor as the European powers sought loans and credits to pay for their war purchases. The three years of neutrality brought enormous wealth to the United States as it both expanded its export trade and lent money to the belligerents. Exports rose from $500 million in 1914 to $3,500 million in 1917. Having begun the war as a debtor country, the United States ended it as the main international lender.

The total direct cost of the war to the United States was around $35.5 billion dollars; this consisted of $24.3 billion of the nation's own expenditure and $11.2 billion in wartime and immediate post-war loans to other nations, mainly the Allies. This was a great deal of money, but the conflict cost the European countries considerably more than this. Moreover, America's national income was roughly $40 billion in 1917 alone and thus it was not too painful for the American people to finance the war. Americans helped to win the war by lending to the government which raised most of the war's cost through bonds rather than taxes. $15.5 billion was raised in bond drives, or Liberty Loans as they became known, while only $8.8 billion was raised through taxation.

It was not clear at the start of the war that it would have such positive effects on the American economy. Initially, the war seemed likely to upset the economy as it interfered with foreign trade and hence tariff revenues. The British naval blockade threatened severe consequences for the American cotton trade since it prevented contact with lucrative Central European markets. Moreover, in September 1914, Secretary of State Bryan, determined to apply the policy of neutrality even-handedly, applied a ban on loans to the belligerents. Potentially this was a major handicap for American trade. The Allies needed credit arrangements to facilitate legal trade. Allied purchases would have been cut drastically if Britain and France had not received substantial credit and loans. Lansing predicted in September 1915 that if the Allies were not given large-scale loans the inevitable result for the United States would be 'restriction of outputs, industrial depression, idle capital, financial demoralisation, and general unrest and suffering among the labouring classes'. However, both of these problems were successfully resolved. In a secret agreement, Britain agreed to buy enough cotton to stabilise the price. As a result, cotton prices rose and a crisis was avoided in the American South. It soon became apparent that the loan ban interfered with the growth of America's war trade and the position on commercial credits softened and later collapsed. Wilson's Secretary of the Treasury, William G. McAdoo, described the war trade as 'lawful and welcome' in August 1915. From the spring of 1915 allied war orders had begun to pour in to American manufacturers and stimulated an industrial boom. Munitions exports increased in value from $40 million in 1914 to $1,290 million in 1916.

By April 1917 American bankers had lent $2,145 million to the Allies (but only $27 million to the Central Powers). In 1934-5 a Senate Committee raised the possibility that the Wilson administration went to war because American bankers feared an allied defeat and needed to protect their loans. Certainly Britain had strained its credit and by late June 1917 had an overdraft of $400 million at the J P Morgan bank. The American ambassador in London sent a cable in March 1917 which concluded that, 'Perhaps our going to war is the only way in which our pre-eminent trade position can be maintained and a panic averted.' Certain New York bankers had strong pro-allied sympathies. Nevertheless, although the United States was deeply involved in the Allies' economic war effort and the Wilson administration was understandably concerned with the health of the American economy, there is no evidence that bankers or munition makers influenced the decision for war. The financial community made great profits in the war years and on the whole favoured continuing peace and neutrality. Moreover, Wilson's goals were more moral and political than economic, although he did hope that economic muscle would give him additional leverage over the Allies. He wrote to Colonel House in July 1917 that, 'England and France have not the same views with regard to the peace that we have by any means. When the war is over we can force them to our way of thinking because by that time they will among other things be financially in our hands.' Such hopes proved to be over-optimistic.

6 American Involvement in the First World War

What difference did American power make in the war? Initially it made very little difference and this was hardly surprising. The German government expected no dramatic reversal of fortunes from US involvement. On 1 April 1917 the American armed forces were insignificant; they could muster 5,791 officers and 121,797 enlisted men. The War Department could have organised a mobile force of only 24,000 and provided only enough ammunition for one and a half days! Despite the politically contentious 'Preparedness' campaign in 1916, military planners had made very few specific preparations for fighting Germany and none for fighting a coalition war against Germany until early 1917. This lack of foresight is difficult to understand, except that Wilson opposed any planning for war during the period of neutrality. German military leaders estimated that it would not be possible to train, equip, and transport any army to Europe in less than 18 months by which time German submarines would have sunk a sufficient amount of allied shipping to have won the war. The mobilisation of a huge army of enormous fighting power and its transport to France just in time to save

Paris and turn back the German advance could not reasonably have been predicted. But this is what, in fact, happened. Between April 1917 and the armistice on 11 November 1918 the United States raised and paid for an army of four million, a navy of 16 new warships and numerous submarines, and an impressive arsenal of modern weapons. Over two million troops arrived in France before the armistice to serve in the American Expeditionary Forces. At a cost of 53,000 killed and 204,000 wounded, the Americans made a significant contribution to the allied victory and justifiably won a place at the peace conference (It is worth noting, however, that the figures were low compared to the approximately 2.3 million battle deaths of British and French troops).

In order to mobilise public opinion in support of the war once America was a participant, Congress established a Committee on Public Information in April 1917. Artists, advertisers, poets, historians, educators, and actors were enlisted in the campaign and the country was inundated with a flood of propaganda pamphlets, posters, and newspapers. Altogether over 100 million pieces of 'literature' were distributed by the committee, whilst 75,000 'four minute men' spoke at cinemas and public meetings. Every 10 days mainly amateur orators received a topic such as 'Why Are We Fighting?' or 'Maintaining Morals and Morale'. Speakers talked on behalf of government departments to convince Americans to conserve food and fuel. During bond drives they sold bonds. The organiser of the Committee, a 40-year-old journalist, George Creel, considered that they had been as effective in the battle at home as the soldiers on the Western Front.

President Wilson at first thought that the main American contribution to the war would be economic and financial, with the navy to help with the U-boat menace, but it soon became clear that US troops were desperately needed. Both Britain and France were teetering on the edge of bankruptcy with their manpower reserves nearly depleted. In April 1917 France suffered a disastrous military setback with the failure of the Nivelle offensive which cost 120,000 casualties and resulted in a series of mutinies within the French army. A British offensive around Passchendaele in November 1917 commanded by General Haig resulted in 300,000 casualties and the gain of a desultory amount of territory. Moreover, Germany now had the spur of defeating the enemy before American reinforcements arrived. They enjoyed a number of successes between April 1917 and the Spring of 1918. Although the Italian army collapsed at Caporetto in October 1917, allowing the Allies to move men to fight in France, this was more than counterbalanced by the results of the success of the Bolshevik Revolution, which led to the defection of Russia from the anti-German coalition and offered Germany the opportunity to transfer at least half a million men to the Western Front. In addition, the German army employed new and effective infantry tactics. The result of their successes was that they advanced to within a few miles of the French capital.

The desperate military situation led the British and French to propose that American units be integrated into existing allied forces but Wilson opposed this suggestion. America was an 'associate', not an ally, of the Entente powers, and the government kept its troops as tightly segregated under American command as a co-ordinated military effort would allow. In February 1918 he instructed Secretary of War Baker that, 'Nothing except sudden and manifest emergency be suffered to interfere with the building up of a great distinct American force at the front, acting under its own flag and officers.' This stance enabled America to maintain the moral high ground and reject the nationalistic aspirations for territorial expansion expressed in the secret treaties and agreements among the Allies. The sense of American 'exceptionalism' that had at first encouraged Wilson to stay out of the conflict also made it appear that the United States fought for nobler aims than the Europeans.

The United States navy and initiatives in the area of shipping made a crucial difference to the outcome of the First World War. The American navy helped to break the grip of the German submarines on transatlantic commerce; its raw materials - food and petroleum in particular - fuelled the Allies spluttering war machine. 600,000 tons of shipping was sunk in March 1917 and an additional 900,000 tons the following month. If that rate of damage had been maintained the Allies could not have continued their war effort for much longer. Following American advice, a convoy system of operating merchant ships in groups was adopted. In this way they could be protected from a submarine attack by an escort of cruisers and destroyers. The Americans implemented a range of other strategies to combat the German submarine menace. The laying of mines threatened to further limit their activities. Although incomplete at the time of the armistice, the Northern Barrage resulted in the laying of over 70,000 mines in the North Sea. Of these, more than 56,000 were American mines laid by the United States Mining Squadron. Working together, the British and American navies established effective control over the shipping lanes between the Western Front and the United States. The navy organised the transportation of troops to France extremely effectively - not a single troop ship was lost to submarines. Moreover, by seizing interned German ships, commandeering neutral ships, taking over all private shipping, constructing new shipyards and building a range of new ships, the Emergency Fleet Corporation established by Congress in April 1917 succeeded in increasing the available tonnage from one million to ten million. For every ship sunk by a U-boat two new ones were built. By the Autumn of 1917 the German submarine menace in the Atlantic was under control - by November sinkings were down to about a third of the April total.

The arrival of the American army probably turned the tide of the war from the middle of 1918. From July 1918, 10,000 troops left America each day and they streamed to the front lines. By November 1918 the

United States had more troops in France than Britain. An American division dramatically and bloodily halted a German advance at Belleau Wood, not far from Paris on 4 June 1918. Winston Churchill later wrote that the French felt that they were present at 'the magical operation of the transfusion of blood'. The military importance of early engagements was not great but the effect on morale was crucial. In mid-July, in what became known as the Second Battle of the Marne, German troops sought to break through at the Chateau Thierry salient. United States troops 275,000 strong, supported the French in stemming a powerful attack. Acting independently, but in close co-operation with the British and French armies, American divisions achieved their objectives in the Meuse-Argonne offensive of September to November 1918 which helped to drive the German army backwards. By the Autumn of 1918 Germany's military leaders were forced to recognise that all hope of victory was gone. In Western Europe, Germany confronted growing allied strength, as American troops and supplies arrived in vast numbers and mounted a powerful counter-offensive. Her allies, Turkey, Bulgaria, and Austria-Hungary began to collapse and to seek peace. The German civilian government, taking advice from their military leaders sued for a peace based upon President Wilson's Fourteen Points speech and other addresses.

7 Conclusion

Elected to the Presidency in 1912 on a platform of domestic reforms, Wilson took office expecting to devote his energies to national issues not international problems. In fact, whilst his domestic successes were considerable, he is remembered chiefly for his success in guiding the United States during its first great modern war and for his dream of ending the threat of future wars through the League of Nations. Wilson's contradictory views on the issues raised by the conflict in Europe between 1914 and 1918 mirrored those of the American people. He spoke eloquently and sincerely in favour of a series of policies which ultimately proved to be incompatible. Some of his most memorable phrases pulled in opposite directions; for example, he talked of America being too proud to fight but insisted on Germany being made to pay for American lives lost, and he was committed to both a peace of compromise and a full allied victory. Nevertheless, Winston Churchill concluded in his history of the First World War, *The World Crisis:*

1 It seems no exaggeration to pronounce that the action of the
  United States with its repercussions on the history of the world
  depended, during the awful period of Armageddon, upon the
  workings of this man's mind and spirit to the exclusion of almost
5 every other factor: and that he played a part in the fate of nations
  incomparably more direct and personal than any other man.

The importance of Woodrow Wilson's personal role in the formulation of foreign policy in this period was undoubted but he was forced into the role of war leader despite himself. The workings of his mind changed over time, often as a reaction to the pressure of events.

Most recent studies of Wilson's presidency praise his handling of foreign relations during the First World War, but it is possible to take a more critical view of his diplomatic and military leadership in this period. In particular, he has been criticised by some historians for a lack of 'realism' in some of his thinking and policy decisions. For example, it is argued that he had little strategic overview of the balance of power in Europe and ignored the potential necessity for American military involvement to preserve it. He failed to educate the American people about the possibility of war and to clarify the dangers of a German victory. In retrospect, historians have seen that American foreign policy needed to accommodate the reality of the increasing global interdependence of the international economy and the existence of world-wide empires. Given the pro-ally nature of American neutrality, it was likely that the USA would enter the conflict at some stage and it has been argued that Wilson should have accepted that fact and planned accordingly. A further charge levelled against Wilson is that he failed to co-ordinate political aims and military strategy. The General Staff had not planned to send an American army abroad. Three years after the beginning of the European war, United States armed forces were still not ready for any more than symbolic involvement. It was over a year before they could make a substantial contribution on the Western Front. The lack of preparedness presented a serious threat to the achievement of the United States' aims. The Bolshevik Revolution in Russia, with its worrying implications for the Eastern Front, opened the possibility of a German victory over the Allies before the Americans could enter the war decisively on the Western Front.

Critics would also argue that Wilson's aims were over-ambitious and unrealistic, and that his actions did not increase the likelihood of their achievement. His belief in America's innocence and uniqueness shaped his vision of the world role of the United States. He projected American ideals of progress and democracy onto the world as the universal basis for permanent peace. He hoped to eliminate the causes of war, not merely to achieve some limited objectives in the current war. Yet his emerging vision of collective security remained essentially unconnected to the deployment of American armed forces. In April 1917 Wilson did not define a national policy towards the specific conflicts in continental Europe. His vision of collective security presupposed that the other nations wanted the same kind of world that America did. In his view, the United States was unselfishly seeking to transcend the old European rivalries and reform the international system - 'There is not a single selfish element, so far as I can see, in the cause we are fighting for. We are fighting for what we believe and wish to be the rights of mankind and for the future peace and security of the world.' He experienced serious difficulties integrating American ideals with European realities. He over-estimated his capacity to transform international relations and exaggerated the power of the United States in 1917 to control international affairs. On a purely practical level, Wilson entered the war without gaining explicit British and French agreement to his war aims.

Whilst a useful corrective to over-sympathetic liberal accounts, realist criticisms of Wilsonian statecraft in the First World War seem harsh and touched with the wisdom of hindsight. Wilson wanted to help reform the world, but he would have settled for protecting the interests of the United States and keeping the nation at peace. His mediation efforts had been sincere. He wanted to keep the United States out by ending the war. During 1917 and 1918 he maintained a delicate balance between aid to the Allies and emphasis upon separate American aims; 'peace without victory' remained his over-riding goal. Even before the United States entered the war Wilson had begun to try to impose his ideas on the shape of the post-war world. In January 1917 he called for 'not a balance of power, but a community of power; not organised rivalries but an organised peace'. He constructed a comprehensive framework that not only recognised the interests of America in global events, but which also assigned it an important voice in determining their course. On the eve of the Paris peace conference, President Wilson could take considerable satisfaction in having contributed decisively to military victory over Germany and in formulating the basis for the peace in his Fourteen Points. At the end of the First World War the people of the United States were faced with a fundamental question - would they accept the world responsibilities which their leader envisaged? Georges Clemenceau, the French premier, is reported to have once remarked cynically, 'God gave us the Ten Commandments, and we broke them. Wilson gave us the Fourteen Points. We shall see'.

Making notes on *'The USA and the First World War'*

Your notes should enable you to understand the following three central themes:
1 Why America stayed out of the First World War, 1914-17.
2 What prompted the decision to enter the European conflict in 1917.
3 How successful and realistic Woodrow Wilson's policies were from 1914 to 1918.

The following list of headings and questions are designed to assist you in ordering your thoughts:

American attitudes towards the war, 1914-17
1.1 Why did America remain neutral at the start of the First World War?
1.2 How easy is it to gauge American public opinion towards the war in Europe?

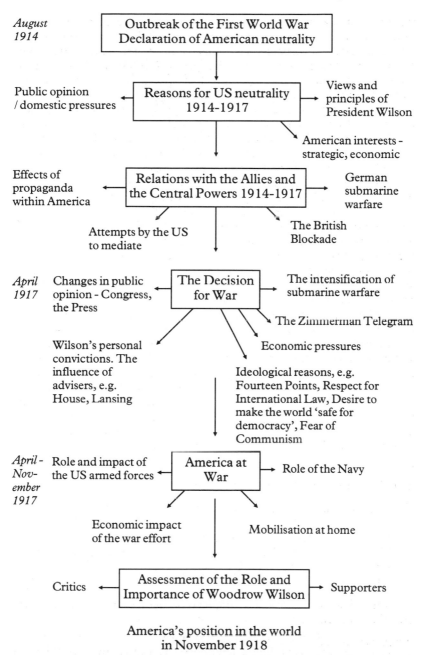

| August 1914 | **Outbreak of the First World War Declaration of American neutrality** |

Public opinion / domestic pressures → **Reasons for US neutrality 1914-1917** ← Views and principles of President Wilson

American interests – strategic, economic

Effects of propaganda within America → **Relations with the Allies and the Central Powers 1914-1917** ← German submarine warfare

Attempts by the US to mediate

The British Blockade

April 1917

Changes in public opinion - Congress, the Press → **The Decision for War** ← The intensification of submarine warfare

The Zimmerman Telegram

Wilson's personal convictions. The influence of advisers, e.g. House, Lansing

Economic pressures

Ideological reasons, e.g. Fourteen Points, Respect for International Law, Desire to make the world 'safe for democracy', Fear of Communism

April - Nov- ember 1917

Role and impact of the US armed forces → **America at War** ← Role of the Navy

Economic impact of the war effort

Mobilisation at home

Critics → **Assessment of the Role and Importance of Woodrow Wilson** ← Supporters

America's position in the world in November 1918

Summary - The USA and the First World War

1.3 How effective was propaganda in favour of the Central Powers?
1.4 Why were the majority of Americans pro-ally in their sentiments?
1.5 In what ways was America affected by German submarine warfare?
1.6 Why did America's neutrality policies work in favour of the Allies?

The Decision for War
2.1 Why did Germany decide to announce unrestricted submarine
     warfare?
2.2 What was the importance of the Zimmerman Telegram?
2.3 What was the justification for America continuing her policy of
     neutrality in March 1917?
2.4 What factors persuaded President Wilson by 2 April 1917 that war
     against Germany was the only honourable course of action?
2.5 What reasons did Wilson give to Congress for his decision?

The Foreign Policy Beliefs and Principles of Woodrow Wilson
3.1 You need to be able to assess the strengths and weaknesses of
     Wilson's handling of foreign relations during the First World War.
     Try drawing up a balance sheet.
3.2 What were the sources of Wilson's principles and advice?
3.3 What were 'Wilsonian principles'?
3.4 How did he pursue peace objectives between 1914 and 1917?
3.5 Where did Wilson get his inspiration for the 'Fourteen Points'?
3.6 What were his aims in announcing his 'Fourteen Points' in January
     1918?

American involvement in the war
4.1 In what ways did the First World War boost the American economy?
4.2 What was the economic relationship between America and the
     Allies?
4.3 What were the main areas in which America contributed to the
     allied victory?
4.4 Why did America describe itself as an 'associate' power?
4.5 How realistic were Wilson's objectives once he had taken America
     into the War?

Answering essay questions on 'The USA and the First World War'

The main focus of questions on this topic is likely to be the reasons why
the United States entered the First World War. The different ways in
which questions are worded, however, means that you need to be
flexible in your thinking and prepared to structure your knowledge and
arguments in direct response to the particular issues to which the
examiner is drawing your attention. It is still a common complaint in
examiners' reports that many candidates fail to address directly the
question they have been asked. The following three questions, for
example, are very similar in the demands which they make of students

but contain subtle differences:

1   Why did President Wilson ask Congress to declare war on Germany in April 1917?
2   Why, and with what aims, did America enter the First World War?
3   Why did the United States follow a policy of neutrality towards Europe in the period 1914-17 and then enter the First World War?

The first question looks in many ways the most straightforward. It might be described as a 'list' essay in that it invites students to think of every possible reason why America went to war (you can find plenty in this chapter) and loosely string them together in paragraph form. If you did this, however, you would be very unlikely to secure the highest grades. On 'why' questions, examiners are usually looking for students to rank factors in order of priority and decide which were the most important reasons. This is a useful task for you to carry out in order to clarify your thinking and start to organise an appropriate paragraph order. Examiners also expect you to zone in and concentrate on the key words of questions - here they would be 'President Wilson', 'Congress', and 'April 1917'. Once you have done this it will become apparent that the question actually contains a whole series of sub-questions. What was President Wilson's personal view of the European conflict? What role did Congress have in the decision to go to war? Why April 1917 and not May 1915 (the sinking of the *Lusitania*) or February 1917 (the publication of the Zimmerman Telegram)? The second question asks you to pay as much attention to America's aims in going to war as to why she went to war. You would need to give approximately equal weight to these two very different issues. The third question pushes you in the direction of explaining America's 'policy of neutrality' in the first two and a half years of the war before looking at the decision for war in April 1917. Again about half your energies should be on the first part of the question and half on the second part.

Another way of posing questions is to suggest that one factor was all important in explaining why a particular decision was taken (or an event occurred) and to challenge the candidate to explain how far they agree with a particular statement or proposition. The following two questions are examples of this style:

4   'Of course, we entered the war simply to maintain the world balance of power'. Is this a satisfactory explanation of the American entry into the First World War?
5   How important was pro-allied sentiment in America prior to 1917 in bringing about the entry of the USA into the First World War?

It goes without saying that there is no 'right' answer to these questions. The best answers will show an awareness that there was a complex range of factors which lay behind the American decision but that one or two reasons were of over-riding importance. They will also support reasoned analysis with plenty of examples and evidence. What would you identify as the key words or phrases in these questions?

One approach to the last question here would be to organise an argument in the following way:

a) Assess the strength of pro-allied sentiment in America 1914-17 and why the majority of American probably supported the 'entente' powers.

b) Emphasise that there were powerful opposing forces within America who favoured Germany. American society was split, Anglo-American relations were sometimes poor.

c) If pro-allied sentiment had been a major factor in bringing American entry into the war it would be reasonable to expect America to have entered the war earlier. The reasons for American neutrality from 1914-1917 thus need to be outlined and explained.

d) Having played down the importance of pro-allied sentiment bringing America into the war, you need to show an awareness of the other possible decisive factors: e.g. unrestricted German submarine warfare, concern for the future European/world balance of power, a growing conviction in Wilson's mind that it was necessary to support the Allies, increasing evidence that America's national interests were directly affected by the conflict, or an ideological/moral desire to uphold democracy.

e) A final paragraph selects one or two of the possible reasons and argues that they were the decisive factor(s) in bringing the entry of the USA into the First World War. My own selection would be unrestricted German submarine warfare and Wilson's changing convictions. Some attention needs to be given to why you give a lower priority to other factors.

This approach is coherent and directly addresses the question. It is not the only or necessarily the 'best' way of answering the question, but it is analytical and comprehensive. The essay would only gain top marks if it provided evidence (key facts, statistics, quotations) to support the generalisations. Try to produce a similar plan of action for Question 4 where you provide an indication of how your arguments would directly address the question.

The main lessons of this advice section are:

1   Read the question carefully. Identify the key words and phrases and establish precisely what the examiner is expecting you to do.

2   When asked the reasons why something has happened, do not simply have a mental list of factors in your head. Rank them in order of priority and reflect that priority in your essay plan.

Source-based Question on 'The USA and the First World War'

1 Cartoon on American neutrality (1915)
Study the cartoon on page 18 and answer the following questions:
a) In what ways does the cartoonist seek to show that the American policy of neutrality was a delicate balancing act? (5 marks)
b) Explain the meaning and motives behind the call 'Hey! I'll have to search you'. (3 marks)
c) How had Wilson demonstrated his 'good intentions' towards Britain and Germany in the first two years of the war? (5 marks)
d) How balanced was the American policy of neutrality? Why was it so difficult to remain truly neutral? (7 marks)

2 Contrasting views on the decision for war in April 1917
Read the extracts from the speeches made in Congress by Woodrow Wilson and Senator La Follette on pages 22-3 and answer the following questions:
a) What do you understand by the phrase 'to vindicate the principles of peace and justice in the life of the world as against selfish and autocratic power'? (4 marks)
b) For what reasons did Senator La Follette oppose Wilson's decision to declare war on Germany? (4 marks)
c) To what extent was La Follette justified in his arguments? (5 marks)
d) How far do you agree that the main element in Wilson's thinking in March 1917 was a desire to make the world 'safe for democracy'? (7 marks)

3 American public opinion and the First World War
Read the section on 'Public Opinion and Neutrality' and also refer to pages 23, 28 and 30.
a) How did President Wilson attempt to gauge the mood of public opinion towards possible American involvement in the First World War? (7 marks)
b) What evidence exists that the policy of neutrality was popular? (4 marks)
c) What is the evidence that public opinion supported the decision to declare war on Germany? (4 marks)
d) What methods were employed to change or alter the attitudes of American people towards the war? (5 marks)

CHAPTER 3

The USA and the Versailles Peace Settlement

1 Introduction

The Paris peace conference opened on 18 January 1919 and lasted until 28 June. The Versailles Settlement is the name given to the series of peace treaties imposed by the victorious Allies of the First World War on the defeated Central Powers (Germany, Austria-Hungary, Bulgaria, and Turkey). The most important part of the settlement was the Treaty of Versailles, concluded with Germany at the end of June 1919. Its main terms were settled during six weeks of hectic negotiations between the 'Big Three' - President Woodrow Wilson of the United States, and Prime Ministers Georges Clemenceau and David Lloyd George for France and Britain. The leaders of Italy and Japan played lesser roles. Each of the participating countries had its own agenda. All sought lasting peace, but they often differed radically about how to achieve it, and their discussions were punctuated by powerful clashes of personality and of national interest.

President Wilson went to Europe in December 1918 to ensure that a new international order, based on the moral principles of the Fourteen Points, would be created via the peace settlement. Ideals such as open diplomacy, freer trade, and national self-determination were to be the essence of an American rejection of isolationism and the entry of the United States into the political affairs of the great powers. Wilson's detailed agenda for the conference contained several issues: territorial adjustments, the treatment of defeated Germany, the relationship of the United States with the victorious Allied powers, the Russian question, and the creation of the League of Nations. In Spring 1918, speaking to a group of foreign correspondents, Wilson had summed up the position of the United States at a future peace conference - 'We come here asking nothing for ourselves and we are here to see that you get nothing.' In the event, the final settlement was generally contrary to the spirit of this statement, especially as it imposed punitive terms on Germany to satisfy the demands of France and Britain. Moreover, the American President failed to secure ratification of the Treaty of Versailles by the American Senate or agreement to American membership of the League of Nations. This chapter seeks to explore some of the reasons why Wilson's hopes were unfulfilled. There is little consensus amongst historians on this topic and it is important to attempt to weigh the opposing arguments which are presented here in the light of the contemporary evidence and additional reading.

2 The Case in Favour of Wilson

The strongest defence of President Wilson rests on a recognition of the breadth and nobility of his aims: his vision of 'a new international order, based upon broad and universal principles of right and justice - no peace of shreds and patches'. A fair-minded peace would help to bring about a harmony of nations' interests and eliminate the conditions which produced war. His aims looked beyond the immediate settlement of issues raised by Germany's defeat. The linked ideas of national self-determination and democracy were to be extended into international relations through a League of Nations. The League was the lynchpin of Wilson's thinking as he sought to harness international law and 'world public opinion'. In the future, rather than resort to militarism, discredited notions of a balance of power, secret alliances, and war, nations would co-exist in peace, submitting differences to arbitration and judicial settlement. He aimed to create a community of independent states 'governed in their conduct towards each other by the same principles of honour and of respect for the common law of civilised society that govern the individual citizens of all modern states in their relations with one another'. Wilson's specific peace aims were set out in a number of speeches which he made in 1917 and 1918 (see pages 22 and 26). The most succinct statement was contained in an address delivered to Congress on 8 January 1918, which is known as the 'Fourteen Points' speech because of the number of headings under which he itemized his peace programme. These were undoubtedly ambitious aims but they were possibly achievable. His programme might have seemed naive to seasoned statesmen and diplomats, but Wilson's faith in a new kind of international order was shared by millions of ordinary people. He was greeted ecstatically by enormous crowds all across Europe in a tour before the peace conference opened which took in London, Paris, Rome, Manchester, and Milan. Two million people greeted Wilson as he entered the French capital. His vision possessed genuine and strong public appeal in Europe.

A Summary of Woodrow Wilson's Fourteen Points

1   Open convenants of peace, openly arrived at, after which there shall be no private international understandings of any kind.
2   Absolute freedom of navigation upon the seas ... in peace and war alike.
3   The removal, so far as possible, of economic barriers.
4   Adequate guarantees given and taken that national armaments be reduced to the lowest point consistent with domestic safety.
5   An open-minded and impartial adjustment of all colonial claims, based upon a strict observance of the principle that the interests of

the population concerned must have equal weight with the equitable claims of the government whose title is to be determined.

6   The evacuation of all Russian territory and ... a settlement of all questions affecting Russia.

7   Belgium ... must be evacuated and restored.

8   All French territory should be freed and the invaded areas restored. The wrong done to France by Prussia in 1871 in the matter of Alsace-Lorraine should be righted.

9   A readjustment of the frontiers of Italy should be effected along clearly recognisable lines of nationality.

10   The peoples of Austria-Hungary ... should be given the freest opportunity for independent development.

11   Rumania, Serbia, and Montenegro should be evacuated by Germany and Austro-Hungarian troops and occupied territories restored; Serbia given free and secure access to the sea. International guarantees of the political and economic independence and territorial integrity of the several Balkan states should be entered into.

12   The Turkish parts of the old Ottoman empire should be assured a secure sovereignty, but the other nationalities under former Turkish rule should be assured an absolutely unmolested opportunity of autonomous development. The Dardanelles should be permanently opened as a free passage to the ships and commerce of all nations under international guarantees.

13   An independent Polish state should be established which should include the territories inhabited by indisputably Polish populations and which should be assured free and secure access to the sea.

14   A general association of nations must be formed under specific covenants for the purposes of affording mutual guarantees of political independence and territorial independence and territorial integrity to great and small states alike.

Article 10 of the League of Nations Covenant:

The Members of the League undertake to respect and preserve as against external aggression the territorial integrity and existing political independence of all Members of the League. In case of any such aggression or in case of any threat or danger of such aggression the Council shall advise upon the means by which this obligation shall be fulfilled.

The American President succeeded in having the covenant of the League of Nations - 'the cornerstone of the peace' as he called it - accepted as an integral part of the treaty. For Wilson, the League lay at the heart of the peacemaking and was the focus of his energies. He believed that it did not matter too much if the terms of the treaty were harsher than he wished because the League would be able to correct any unfairnesses later.

1 If that objective can be safely reached we can afford to allow a number of decisions to be made touching the reconstruction of Europe which might neither meet with my approval nor correspond with what a strictly impartial judge would consider
5 proper. It will be the business of the League to set such matters right.

Wilson chaired and dominated most of the meetings of the League of Nations Commission. At the outset, it was by no means certain that the final covenant would reflect Wilson's ideas and convictions. The Commission started with a draft structure for a future League which was largely based on the British policy of the organisation being dominated by the great powers. However, after much discussion, the structure that was finally agreed was close to the ideals of the American President. For example, four smaller powers were to be represented on the Council of the League in keeping with Wilson's principle of the equality of nations, and the Charter had a significant social dimension - a new International Labour Organisation promised to improve working and living conditions for men, women, and children. Article 10 offered a mutual guarantee of territorial integrity and political independence for all nations in the new League, whilst Article 19 anticipated adjustments to agreements reached at Versailles. Wilson's finest hour at Paris came on 14 February when he presented the Covenant to a plenary session of the conference:

this document ... is not a straitjacket, but a vehicle of life. A living thing is born ... it is at one and the same time a practical document and a humane document ...

Wilson returned home to America on 23 February to attend briefly to some important domestic business, having enjoyed a successful first phase of the conference.

Wilson was later criticised for his decision to attend the peace conference in person and to take an active part in the deliberations. In recent times presidential 'summitry' is taken for granted but such a journey was something new in 1918. Nevertheless, Wilson's decision was justifiable. He was convinced that the defence of his principles and a duty to the American war-dead required his presence. Moreover, he felt that only his prestige as President could force the victorious allied powers to accept the peace which he sought. Wilson had good reason not fully to trust his subordinates. Lansing, the Secretary of State was a sound and thoughtful lawyer but lacked real political weight and Wilson regularly discounted his advice. In Lloyd George's view 'he just did what he was told, and was never told to do very much'. Colonel House was a subtle and effective diplomat but too prone to compromise on important issues in Wilson's absence. Wilson's biographer, Ray Stannard Baker, described House as 'a matchless conciliator, but with all the faults of his virtue, for he conciliates over the border of minor disagreements into the solid flesh of principle'. Wilson complained to his wife on his return to the conference from America that 'House has given away everything I had won before we left.' Arguably, too, Wilson was justified in his partisan approach to the choice of leading American delegates to the conference. He chose House, Lansing, Tasker Bliss who had been the American military representative on the supreme War Council, and a lone Republican, the retired diplomat Henry White. He ignored the claims of prominent Republicans such as former President Taft, Elihu Root, Charles Edward Hughes, or Henry Cabot Lodge. This was because leading Republicans had adopted a highly partisan approach to the Congressional elections in November 1918. Taft, as Chairman of the League to Enforce Peace organisation, was most often cited as a suitable delegate, but he had campaigned through three north-east states denouncing Wilson's Fourteen Points. In his view they could not 'be made the safe basis of a treaty of peace. They are too vague and indefinite'.

It is important to emphasise the domestic constraints and pressures which tended to undermine Wilson's authority in Paris and weakened his negotiating hand. The Congressional elections in November 1918 transformed Democratic majorities in the House of Representatives and Senate into Republican majorities of 26 and 2 seats respectively. The elections should not necessarily be read as a national poll on Wilson's leadership. Mid-term elections often go against the party in power and domestic issues such as taxation and the price of wheat were at least as important as foreign policy issues. A number of the Republican victories were by very narrow margins. Nevertheless, as Lloyd George pointed out, the electoral setback damaged Wilson:

1 [it] undoubtedly lowered his prestige and crippled his authority
  throughout the conference ... It also unconsciously impaired his
  own confidence. He could take no unnecessary risks in the way of
  insistence on his own point of view. His occasional threats to
5 appeal to American opinion, when he did not get his way at the
  conference, conveyed no real menace.

Before Wilson crossed the Atlantic in December 1918, ex-President Theodore Roosevelt had asserted that the Allies were entitled to impose whatever peace they chose. He denied that Wilson, his Points, Principles, or Particulars 'have any shadow of right to be accepted as expressive of the will of the American people'. More damagingly, on the eve of Wilson's re-embarkation for Europe, on 3 March 1919, a resolution sponsored by Henry Cabot Lodge the Chairman of the Senate Foreign Relations Committee, openly rejected the covenant of the League of Nations as contrary to the Monroe Doctrine. It was signed by 39 Republican senators. This so-called 'Round Robin' resolution served notice that at least a third of the Senate would probably vote not to ratify the peace treaty as it stood. This would be sufficient to prevent acceptance of the treaty. The need to seek concessions on the structure of the League to meet some of the Senate's concerns weakened Wilson's bargaining position in other areas of contention. In effect the Allies took the League of Nations hostage and presented ransom notes seeking American concessions on territory (notably the Saar area and the Rhineland) and reparations.

The President was well-prepared for the negotiations in Paris and aware of the complexity of many of the issues involved. In September 1917 Wilson had asked House to seek out experts who would study the probable issues of the peace conference and recommend 'what influences we can use to achieve American goals'. House put together a group of experts known as 'The Inquiry'. He took a large and well-qualified support staff with him to Paris. Harold Nicolson commented that the ship on which the American party travelled 'creaked and groaned across the Atlantic under the weight of their erudition' and added that he had 'never had to work with a body of men more intelligent, more scholarly, more broad-minded or more accurately informed than were the American delegation'. Wilson used their reports extensively. John Maynard Keynes, who had served as a British treasury official at the conference until he quit in disgust in June 1919, famously depicted Wilson in his 1920 book, *The Economic Consequences of the Peace*, as slow-witted and bamboozled by his European colleagues, but this was unfair. Nicolson commented in contrast that 'as compared with his colleagues at the Council table, Mr. Wilson was fully practical, admirably informed, perfectly precise'. Moreover, Wilson often received contradictory recommendations from various groups within his delegation.

Given the scale of the problems facing the peacemakers at Versailles, Wilson was always likely to disappoint his admirers whose expectations were beyond anybody's power to achieve. As far as they were concerned, the task was nothing less than to reshape the world, the nature of states, and international relations in a new image. Keynes commented that President Wilson 'enjoyed a prestige and moral influence unequalled throughout history', and that 'never had a philosopher held such weapons wherewith to bind the princes of this world', but he exaggerated Wilson's power.

In considering the effectiveness of American diplomacy it is important to note that Britain and France had suffered respectively some 900,000 and 1.4 million battle deaths in the war - 47 times as many as the United States - and therefore felt that they had more right to influence the terms of the peace than did America. Moreover, the Fourteen Points did not yield clearcut and detailed solutions to particular problems. For example, the principle of self-determination was enormously difficult to apply, particularly in Central and Eastern Europe where the races were so intermingled that no conceivable rearrangement of frontiers could do justice to all. There was a mass of detail to untangle. Should a linguistic frontier be severed in order to accommodate an existing rail link? Should a mining area, vital to the economies of neighbouring nationalities be divided and dislocated? 'What more could I have done?', Wilson asked a historian interviewing him in January 1921, 'I had to negotiate with my back to the wall. Men thought I had all power. Would to God I had had such power. The 'great' people at home wrote and wired every day that they were against me.'

Compromise at Paris was inevitable and necessary. Differences between the Allies over the interpretation of the Fourteen Points emerged even before the conference opened, as Britain insisted on opting out of the provision relating to 'freedom of the seas' and France insisted on the necessity of Germany paying substantial reparations. The news blackout, which Wilson allowed himself to be talked into, denied the world the opportunity to understand the difficulty of the issues and the reasons for compromise. Decisions had to be taken, on many occasions, with imperfect information, under pressure, when those responsible were both physically and mentally exhausted. Wilson faced appalling alternatives if he had failed to compromise. On all sides his Points and Principles were under sustained attack. Yet if he stood up for his principles, as he showed himself willing and able to do, he seemed likely to bring about the break-up of the conference (indeed, weary of allied obstruction, on 6 April Wilson ordered that a ship be made ready to take him home). The success of communist revolutions in Europe added considerable urgency to the situation. Following the Bolshevik Revolution in Russia, Western leaders feared that communism, feeding on defeat, destruction, and hunger would engulf all of Europe. During the summer and autumn of 1918 the collapse of the Russian, German, and Austro-Hungarian military power left Central Europe in chaos. Hungary established a communist government under Bela Kun in March 1919 which lasted five months, and strong communist movements appeared in Poland and Germany. Thus, as Colonel House put it, 'It was sometimes necessary to compromise in order to get things through ... not a compromise of principle but a compromise of detail.' Delay risked revolution. House noted in his diary, 'If the world were not in such a fluid state I should not object to matters going as deliberately as they have been going; but under present conditions we are gambling each day with the situation.' If Wilson had bolted and gone home he might have thrown Europe into still greater turmoil - the honourable course was to 'get the best treaty possible under the circumstances'.

Italian and Japanese territorial ambitions exemplified the pressures upon Wilson's principles. With respect to the former, Wilson argued that the Treaty of London (1915) which had promised Italy territorial annexations had been intended only to protect Italy from the Austro-Hungarian Empire. With the Empire gone, the treaty should be superseded by the principle of self-determination. In particular, Wilson objected to Italy being granted Fiume on the Dalmatian coast. In pique, the Italian Prime Minister, Orlando, withdrew from the conference from 21 April until 7 May. Japan failed in an attempt to get an article on racial equality inserted into the covenant of the League of Nations. This failure increased her leverage elsewhere. She was determined to obtain Germany's economic rights and concessions in the Shantung province of China. This claim was validated by secret treaties signed with Britain and France in February and March 1917. In this case Wilson compromised. He told Stannard Baker, 'They are not bluffers, and they will go home unless we give them what they should not have.' He described the deal, which contained the verbal promise that Japan would respect Chinese sovereignty in the long run, as 'the best that could be accomplished out of a dirty past'. If both Italy and Japan had deserted the peace conference the League of Nations would have been shattered from the start.

Recent research emphasises the President's poor health at the conference which may have impaired his judgement. Many historians accept the conclusions of pioneering medical biographies - there is agreement that Wilson suffered from long-standing hypertension, carotid artery disease, and progressive cerebrovascular disease or 'premature old age'. Long before he reached the White House, Wilson may have suffered at least two strokes; in 1896 he suddenly lost control in his right hand, whilst in 1906 he awoke blind in his left eye, subsequently recovering some but not full vision. Based upon the analysis of new records released by the family of Wilson's doctor, the President's brief illness during the peace conference has been diagnosed as probably a minor stroke. His physical exhaustion was undoubted. He was used to working a three to four hour day with plenty of relaxation. At Paris Wilson spent hours in meetings, the League of Nations Commission, private meetings with the leaders of the smaller nations and briefings with his own delegation. Moreover, his apartment was besieged daily by representatives of innumerable nationalities who wished to plead their case with Wilson in person. Greeks, Albanians, Lithuanians, Poles, Jews, Irishmen, and many others beat a path to his door. His voice grew hoarse, he developed a nervous facial tic, his hair grew white, and he began to suffer severe headaches. Therefore, there is convincing evidence that his illness in late March and early April, on top of previous vascular disease, had a serious effect on Wilson's physical and perhaps mental strength. Several of the compromises with the Fourteen Points that later alienated the President's liberal supporters took place in this period. He accepted the 'War Guilt' clauses, the Anglo-French position on reparations, the French demand for a 15 year occupation of the Rhineland, and French control of the Saar coal mines, all of which represented considerable shifts from his earlier positions.

The Versailles peace settlement was not a complete rejection of Wilsonianism - arguably it was a modification rather than a repudiation of the Fourteen Points. The peace was fairer than it would have been without Wilson's intervention. Without his efforts many of the 440 terms of the peace settlement would have been far more severe. The territorial provisions were not as bad as disillusioned contemporaries believed. The recognition of Poland, Yugoslavia, Czechoslovakia, and other nation states in Central Europe satisfied many people. Germany was not partitioned despite the fact that the French government made a major effect to achieve this by establishing the Rhineland area as an autonomous state under the control of France. The concept of stewardship of mandates under international supervision rather than colonial rule may not have always worked out well in practice but morally it implied that exploitation of one people by another was wrong and proclaimed the ideal of independence for all peoples - in other words a significant if incomplete victory for Wilson's principles. Considering the diplomatic realities which constrained him, Wilson probably infused the covenant of the League of Nations with as progressive a character as possible. The settlement might be viewed as an honest effort to accommodate nationalism but also to establish a mechanism within which nationalist ambitions could be established peacefully. Wilson admitted that the treaty was 'far from ideal' but argued that it was 'tolerably close to the lines laid down at the outset'. House concluded that 'While I should have preferred a different peace, I doubt whether it could have been made.'

The Terms of the Treaty of Versailles

- Germany was deprived of over 10 per cent of her pre-war territory, population, and economic resources, particularly coal and iron.
- Alsace-Lorraine was returned to France.
- A small border strip, Eupen-Malmedy, was given to Belgium.
- Northern Schleswig went to Denmark.
- To the newly created Poland was transferred the province of Posen and the so-called 'Polish Corridor', both German territory for over a century and containing large German populations. The 'Polish Corridor' cut off East Prussia from the rest of Germany.
- The German port of Danzig became a 'free city' administered by

the League of Nations in order to secure Poland's promised access to the Baltic.
- The industrial area of Upper Silesia was divided between Poland and Germany in 1922 after a plebiscite which Germany considered unfair.
- Germany lost all of her overseas colonies.
- The Rhineland, consisting of all German territory on the Left bank of the river Rhine and a 50 kilometre strip along the right bank became a 'de-militarized zone', permanently out of bounds to German troops. The left bank was to remain under Allied occupation for a maximum of 15 years.
- France was granted ownership of the Saar coalmines for 15 years. The Saarland area was to be administered by the League of Nations for the same period, its subsequent future to be decided by a plebiscite.
- Germany was required to disarm and to limit her armed forces to a volunteer defence force of 100,000 and a small navy.
- Germany bound herself to pay reparations to the Allies, particularly Britain and France.
- Under Article 231, the 'War-Guilt clause', Germany was forced to accept responsibility for the war, which was attributed to her aggression.

3 The Case Against Wilson

The strongest criticism of the American President is that he proved unable to implement American principles as represented in his Fourteen Points. He was unable to prevent the grabbing for money and land by the victorious European powers that had discredited peace settlements in the past. Wilson saw it as his first and most difficult task to make the leaders of Britain, France, Italy, and other participating countries see that the treaty 'must not be a peace of loot or spoliation'. He wanted 'no annexations and no indemnities'. The German government agreed to a ceasefire in November 1918 on the basis of the Fourteen Points and the American President promised the German people 'full, impartial justice'. As it turned out, the golden vision of a 'Wilson Peace' faded into a nightmare of compromise and tactical manoeuvring and the settlement became an object of later shame and regret. When the terms of the settlement were announced German representatives pointed out the inconsistencies between the draft treaty and the Fourteen Points and demonstrated with shocking directness that the President had betrayed his principles. Several of the young and previously hopeful members of the American delegation resigned in protest at the harshness of the peace. One complained that America had 'bartered away her principles in a series of compromises with the interests of imperialism and revenge'. In Clemenceau's view 'Wilson talked like Jesus Christ but acted like Lloyd George'.

The British Prime Minister commented in his account of the negotiations in Paris:

1   Those who view the treaty as a cauldron of hatred, revenge, and rapacity, but find it difficult to know where to place President Wilson on that assumption, picture him as the poor dupe of a couple of expert political gunmen who alternately bullied and 5   cajoled, hoodwinked and flattered him until the poor man ultimately signed on the dotted line.

Although he rejected this interpretation, it contained significant elements of truth. Keynes' eyewitness account described Wilson as old, slow, and ignorant, combining dithering incompetence with mental rigidity and spiritual arrogance. Wilson was ultimately defeated by 'the swift arrows of Clemenceau's Latin intellect, with the kingfisher dartings of Lloyd George's intuition'. Colonel House, himself a master of the political deal, described the British and French leaders as the two most skilled negotiators he had ever seen. In some ways the outcome of the negotiations might be seen as a distinctly personal failure by Wilson. Certainly Keynes was savage- 'He had no plan, no scheme, no constructive ideas whatever for clothing with the flesh of life the commandments which he had thundered from the White House'.

The decision to attend and participate in the detailed negotiations of the peace settlement in person turned out to be a mistake. When, as House put it, 'He stepped from his lofty pedestal and wrangled with representatives of other states upon equal terms, he became as common clay.' He forfeited one of his strongest weapons - that of mystery, uncertainty, and distant authority. Secretary of State Lansing confided to his diary after hearing that Wilson intended travelling to Paris, that the President was 'making one of the greatest mistakes of his career and imperilling his reputation'. Wilson's private secretary, Joseph Tumulty, and his personal doctor also advised against attendance. He might have maintained the integrity of his principles more effectively away from the quagmire of compromise into which he was drawn. If Wilson had remained in Washington he would, of necessity, have given his representatives written instructions, which would have provided a more solid basis for negotiations than ever existed with him present. He would also have been able to stay in touch with congressional and public opinion. Staying at home would have allowed him to take the credit for perceived successes and to disown inconvenient agreements. Harold Nicolson viewed Wilson's presence in Paris as a considerable misfortune; 'The collapse of Wilson meant the collapse of the conference .... His presence in Paris constitutes a historical disaster of the first magnitude'.

Wilson did little to shore up a weakening position on the domestic front and this in turn weakened his authority in Paris. He made an ill-advised attempt near the end of the 1918 congressional election campaign to turn the poll into a personal vote of confidence. He appealed to the electorate (in vain) to return a Democratic Congress. This was probably a mistake; historically Presidents have better served their own and their parties' interests by limiting their involvement in mid-term elections. Subsequently, the glaring exclusion from the American delegation of any prominent Republican clouded the prospects for Senate ratification of a Wilsonian peace. One of the reasons that Wilson refused to nominate a leading Republican such as Taft, Root, or Senator Philander C. Knox, a former Secretary of State, was that none of them would have subordinated himself to the presidential will. Wilson did not treat his immediate predecessor, Taft, with the consideration he deserved. He might have used the predominantly Republican League to Enforce Peace to counter American critics of the League of Nations. Indeed, after the armistice he should have sought to discover how much domestic support his new ideas might have. By discouraging discussion of the possible structure and aims of the League of Nations, Wilson deprived himself of the benefit of having an American consensus behind him in Paris and put the Senate in the position of having to take or leave an accomplished fact. There was a post-war reaction in America against foreign entanglements and an unease about the yet greater responsibilities which the President sought to thrust upon the American people. To Wilson, however, defeat was unthinkable. He stopped listening and misread Congress and the mood of the American people.

The American President can also be criticised for a lack of system and method in his planning for the conference and his failure to consult more widely. Wilson may have set up 'The Inquiry' and had plenty of technical advice to call upon in Paris, but, apart from on economic questions, he largely ignored the reams of paper churned out by his experts. 'Tell me what is right and I will fight for it,' he had told his delegation on the way to Europe. In fact, Secretary of State Lansing had wanted to prepare a skeleton treaty for the guidance of the American delegation but Wilson brushed him aside with the curt and insulting remark that he did not intend to have lawyers drafting the treaty of peace. Thus, whilst the Europeans came with concrete proposals, Wilson sought general solutions. Even with respect to the League of Nations, Wilson's ideas were vague. He relied on drafts of mainly British origin for its structure. He proposed that the conference grant mandates to run the colonies of the defeated countries, yet relied upon the imperial representatives' proposals for the structure of the mandates. The British were not expecting a master of detail, but they did not expect him to be as casual as he was. Lansing, bitter at being frozen out of the negotiations, was later sharply critical of Wilson's handling of the conference proceedings. An atmosphere of uncertainty prevented the American delegation from pressing for definite objects.

1 The consequence was that the general scheme of the treaty and
   many of the important articles were prepared and worked out by
   the British and French delegations. Thus the exceptional
   opportunity which the President had to impress his ideas on the
5 conference and to lead in the negotiations was lost, and he failed to
   maintain his controlling position among the statesmen who were as
   it turned out to dictate the terms of peace ... He was inclined to let
   matters drift, relying apparently on his own quickness of
   perception and his own sagacity to defeat or amend terms
10 proposed by members of other delegations. From first to last there
   was no team work, no common counsel, and no concerted action.

If Wilson was overworked then he should take some of the blame for a failure to delegate. He preferred to retain a self-righteous belief in his own judgement. Lansing again put it in acid terms - 'His judgements were always right in his own mind because he knew they were right. How did he know they were right? Why, he *knew* it, and that was the best reason in the world.'

The peace settlement is most easily considered as the negotiation of a succession of compromises between the victorious powers. Nevertheless, there is a strong case for arguing that the American President capitulated (rather than the three main participants giving ground in equal amounts) in too many key areas. The initiative at the beginning of the conference lay with the United States, which had been able to end the war with both sides apparently agreeing to its peace programme as a result of the 'armistice contract' of November 1918. Britain and France had sought clarification of the Fourteen Points and an allied memorandum subsequently known as the Lansing Note contained a significant qualification of Wilson's principles. It noted that 'the Allied Governments feel that no doubt ought to be allowed to exist' as to the demands to be made of Germany. By the President's stipulation in regard to restoration; they understood that 'compensation will be paid by Germany for all damage done to the civilian population of the Allies and their property by the aggression of Germany by land, by sea, and from the air'. There was no mention here of reparations for the cost of prosecuting the war (to the dismay of British Dominions such as Australia). Wilson did not seek reparation from Germany, although it should be added that he refused to cancel the colossal war-debts owed to America by Britain and France. Early in the conference, Wilson held to the line that the inclusion of war costs was contrary to the pledge given to Germany before the signing of the armistice, but Lloyd George sought to wriggle away from the terms of the Lansing Note (Wilson once commented to his doctor of the British Prime Minister, 'he is as slippery as an eel and I never know when to count on him'). In a clever manoeuvre, Lloyd George looked at disability pensions as a chance to increase Britain's share of the spoils. A soldier discharged as unfit through enemy action became a civilian and his injury could therefore be seen as 'civilian damage'. Persuaded by Jan Smuts, the South African representative, whose opinion, according to House, the President valued 'more highly than that of any other person in the British delegation', Wilson caved in. When some of his own experts criticised him for departing from the logic of the Pre-Armistice Agreement, the President exclaimed 'I don't give a damn for logic. I am going to include pensions!'. The conference passed the total reparations bill to a commission that in 1921 asked Germany for $33 billion. The scale of the financial penalty imposed upon Germany created lasting resentment and was to be a major cause of international economic instability throughout the 1920s and early 1930s..

The compromises Wilson was prepared to make over the principle of self-determination were even more marked. The principle was applied with great elasticity. Lansing commented half way through the conference that the 'game of grab goes merrily on' with every European nation trying to get every foot of territory and every economic advantage'. 'It really disgusts one to see what is being attempted'. Many of the attempts succeeded. Moreover, the ambitions of the great powers were mirrored and exceeded by the greediness of the lesser states. The Polish leader insisted, for example, on the port of Danzig as a pledge of Poland's promised 'free and secure access to the sea' and a corridor of German land to reach the port. Nor was it only European countries involved in the 'game of grab'; Japan and Australia clung to their spoils in the Pacific. The war had undermined the moral authority of European colonial rule in Africa, the Middle East, and Asia, but Wilson acquiesced in a 'mandate' system which effectively carved up Germany's colonial empire between the victors with the League of Nations legitimating their title. From early April 1919 Wilson compromised his principal of self-determination at almost every turn. Examples included the awards to Italy of the South Tyrol, the Saar coal mines to France, the Sudetenland to Czechoslovakia, and Hungarian Transylvania to Romania. The decisions provoked demoralisation amongst the Presidential entourage. It now seemed not only that Wilson no longer meant what he said but that all too often he did not know what he was talking about. He was ignorant when he made many of these promises that he was allowing annexation and, for example, was unaware that the population of the South Tyrol was Austrian or that the new boundaries of Czechoslovakia contained three million Germans.

For many weeks Wilson held firm to the vision of a just peace, then, physically exhausted, hounded by the French press, and frustrated with continually countering practical demands with lofty principles, his resolve collapsed. In early April, confined to his room, Wilson threatened to leave the conference 'unless peace was made according to their promises, which were to conform to the principles of the Fourteen Points'. To Mrs Wilson he is reported to have said, 'I can never sign a treaty made on these lines and if all the rest of the delegates have determined on this, I will not be a party to it. If I have lost my fight which I would not have done had I been on my feet, I will retire in good order; so we will go home.' The threat was not carried through. Ray Stannard Baker, Wilson's biographer and press secretary, would have preferred that he go down fighting at the Peace conference and not yield. 'It would be better for him and for the principles - for the world - in the long run,' he wrote in his diary in April 1919. He was inconsistent in the application of his principles - for example, he displayed an inflexible insistence upon the principle of self-determination in dealing with the Italian claims to the Dalmatian Coast which contrasted with his handling of Japanese claims in the same period. He also seemed to become stubborn and uncompromising at precisely the wrong moments. For example, late in the conference there was disagreement over the question of Upper Silesia an important mining area in Central Europe. The area had been allocated to Poland despite the preponderance of German speakers. Under domestic pressure to ease some of the terms of the settlement, Lloyd George argued in defence of Wilson's principles, calling for a plebiscite to allow the local population to determine for themselves whether they lived under German or Polish rule. Wilson refused to amend the treaty. 'Cannot understand Wilson', wrote Harold Nicolson, 'Here is a chance of improving the thing and he won't take it'. Wilson sadly refused to believe that he had compromised his principles. He believed that he had 'only learned discretion'. He spoke of reconciling idealism with 'realpolitik'. He clung to the idea that the League of Nations would overcome all unwelcome compromises in the treaty.

4 The Treaty Fight in the Senate

a) Introduction

Wilson was confident that he could win the support of the American people and Senate approval for the settlement he had negotiated in Paris and American membership of the League of Nations. There were good reasons for his optimism: 32 state legislatures had endorsed the covenant of the League of Nations, 33 state governors had expressed approval, and a poll of 1,377 newspaper editors found that a vast majority (including a majority of Republican papers) advocated American membership of the League, with only 181 irreconcilably opposed. Nevertheless, Wilson was expecting a fight with his domestic opponents. Before he left Paris, House urged the President to compromise with his critics in the Senate and Wilson is said to have replied, 'I have found that you can never get anything in this life that is worthwhile without fighting for it.' He confided to the American ambassador to Britain that as soon as the conference ended he was going home to 'lick those fellows in the Senate'. In a speech outlining the terms of the settlement to the Senate on 10 July 1919 he urged unqualified approval - 'Shall we or any other free people hesitate to accept this great duty? Dare we reject it and break the heart of the world?'

In fact, Wilson overestimated his personal powers of persuasion and the Senate did reject the treaty - a verdict few would have predicted in the summer of 1919. Complete rejection of the treaty and the League of Nations was an outcome no-one except the so-called 'irreconcilables' wanted. The Senate's consideration of the issues and debates on the treaty lasted between July 1919 and the spring of 1920 which was longer than the Paris conference itself. Wilson's determination to compel the Senate to approve the treaty without any reservations encountered widespread Republican resistance. The Republicans enjoyed only a slim majority with 49 seats - 2 more than the Democrats - but the two vote majority allowed them to pack key committees with 'strong reservationists' and control the administrative machinery of the Senate.

Henry Cabot Lodge of Massachusetts ensured that there was a 'strong reservationist' majority on the influential Senate Foreign Relations Committee of which he was the chairman. A sufficient number of senators in successive votes rejected the settlement so that it could not be passed by the necessary two-thirds majority. The mathematics of the balance in the Senate was that the Democrats needed to secure about 20 Republican votes in order to gain a two thirds majority. Thus they had to win the support not only of the 10 or so 'mild reservationists'; on the Republican side who favoured the treaty with minor changes, but also 10 more Republicans. Reservations were the central issue in the Senate's debate over acceptance of the treaty. The Republican majority, joined by a few Democrats, proposed reservations to define and limit the role of the United States under the terms of the settlement. There was a distinction between reservations and amendments; an amendment would have required renegotiation with the Allies but a reservation did not change the text and other nations could accept it without formal acknowledgement. Nevertheless, the critical reservations relating to Article 10 of the League of Nations would have effectively given the Americans an opt-out clause. Lodge's proposal would have required majority approval by Congress in order to participate in actions agreed by the League's Council, especially economic sanctions and the use of military force. As it turned out, President Wilson not only failed to realise his vision of collective security but ultimately witnessed the Senate's rejection of both the peace treaty and American membership of the League. It is hard to imagine a less constructive outcome to the domestic debate over the peace treaty than that which occurred in 1920. The United States exercised the greatest economic and potential military power in the world in 1919-20 but Americans showed an apparent unwillingness to play a larger more committed role in world affairs.

   Historians' interpretations and explanations for the rejection vary in their focus. Early accounts focused on the personal antagonism between Wilson and Lodge and were critical of the partisanship which became increasingly evident in the exchanges and arguments. Others emphasised Wilson's stubbornness in the face of overwhelming odds. Most critics would argue that League membership, even under strict reservations, was a worthy half loaf which would have ensured a more active American role in world affairs. More sympathetic historians relate Wilson's unwillingness or inability to compromise with his senatorial opponents to his poor health. Wilson suffered a major stroke on 2 October 1919 at a critical point in the Senate's consideration of the treaty. For a week he lay close to death and he remained almost completely isolated from outside contacts for over three months. The treaty debate would almost certainly have gone better if Wilson had died in the autumn of 1919. A wave of national remorse might have driven reluctant senators to approve a treaty with few reservations. Perhaps a healthy Wilson would have found a way to accommodate the reservationists. As it was, his poor health deepened his intransigence. Other historians see the League fight as a fundamental debate over the essence of American foreign policy - whether it would commit itself to collective security or opt for unilateralism (in other words, decide upon intervention on the individual merits of each case depending upon American national interests). It was 'easy to talk about a League of Nations and the beauty and necessity of peace', Lodge remarked, 'But the hard practical demand is, are you ready to put your soldiers and sailors at the disposition of other nations?'

5 Opponents of the Treaty

a) The Irreconcilables

There were 16 senators - 14 Republicans and two Democrats - who fought for complete rejection of the treaty irrespective of any qualifying reservations. Most had come out against League membership soon after the covenant was published. They were a diverse group united only in their conviction that the treaty must be defeated not in the nature of their conviction or their degree of opposition. There was a geographical spread of representation with five from the East, five from the West, and six representing Mid-West states. Some of these senators had narrow and prejudiced agendas - 'bungalow minds' was a Wilson expression. Thus, for example, James Reed, a Democrat senator from Missouri emphasised the racial peril of this 'coloured League of Nations', observing that its initial membership included only 15 white nations but

17 'black, brown, yellow, and red races'. He feared these nations would use their majority to the detriment of 'civilized government'. James Sherman (Illinois) stressed that the League would include 17 Catholic nations but only 11 Protestant countries and 4 other faiths - consequently the Pope would control a majority of the members. In general, however, it is unfair to see them as ignorant traditionalists. Although only a small bloc, they were intelligently led by influential figures such as William Borah (Idaho), Hiram Johnson (California), and Philander Knox (Pennsylvania). They wished to continue America's policy of abstention from international commitments and maintained a fundamental belief in American autonomy. America should be the sole commander of its destiny, unentangled. Some believed that the treaty betrayed the idealism of the 14 Points; most believed that the treaty was too idealistic and unrealistic.

As a group the irreconcilables or 'bitter-enders' achieved a number of tactical successes. They helped to devise the Round Robin resolution of February 1919 which helped to force Wilson to make changes in the original covenant, their formation of an anti-League propaganda organization, and their delaying tactics all contributed to the treaty's defeat. Above all they grasped the nature of the parliamentary struggle which confronted them. Finding it impossible to obtain a Senate majority for outright rejection of the treaty they worked with Lodge to adopt reservations the President found unacceptable. Their views coincided with a growing mood of apathy or hostility on the part of many citizens towards membership of the League of Nations - there was a weariness of crusades, idealism, and European distresses - and problems enough at home. For such citizens it was wrong that American sovereignty be diminished by membership of a League superstate. The sacred Monroe Doctrine should not be weakened and the United States should preserve full freedom to follow its own interests and regulate its own affairs.

b) Lodge and the Strong Reservationists

The largest group of Republican senators were strong reservationists; in other words they did not irreconcilably oppose the peace settlement but insisted upon certain reservations before they supported it. The spokesman for this group was Henry Cabot Lodge, the Senate majority leader. Lodge's role in the treaty debates marked the high point of his long career. He was an experienced politician who had built up legislative skills over three decades in Washington. Like Wilson he had engaged in scholarly study and writing about American history and international relations. He was a strong partisan who had been critical of Wilson's foreign policy from the outset of the administration, claiming that its chief characteristics were 'feebleness and ignorance'. By 1915 he could comment to Theodore Roosevelt that he 'never expected to hate anyone in politics with the hatred I feel towards Wilson'. He detested the President for 'his utter indifference to principle, his lack of generous emotion, his entire subjection to his own personal animosities and his deep-rooted timidity'. The Democratic Platform in the 1920 Presidential election campaign later created the myth that the Republican Senate 'interposing partisan envy and personal hatred in the way of the peace and prosperity of the world' had refused to ratify the treaty 'merely because it was the product of Democratic statesmanship'. In truth, it was relatively easy to demonise Lodge who lacked charisma and sympathetic characteristics - even an admirer commented that he 'managed to impress people as a rather cynical opportunist at best'. Nevertheless, it is unnecessary to attack the motives and character of those who opposed Wilson and unfair to depict Lodge as the villain of the piece. There were considerable practical and political difficulties involved in the construction of a system to enforce peace. The nub of the problem was that Americans could not agree upon the nature of the League they wanted nor upon the arrangements to make it work.

Two goals were uppermost in Lodge's mind - Republican unity and securing American participation in international affairs on what he regarded as a sound basis of national interests. He achieved the first goal by putting together a package of reservations that satisfied the majority of Republicans inside and outside the Senate. Specifically, strong reservationist senators wanted guarantees of American superiority in the Western hemisphere and opposed Article 10 of the League covenant. Moreover, whilst Wilson viewed the conduct of American foreign relations as primarily a presidential function, Lodge and his Republican colleagues asserted the rights of Congress. Lodge was less successful in respect of his second goal. According to his most recent biographer, in dealing with the various blocs of Republican opinion Lodge 'had to be less than forthright in expressing his own views, had often to be all things to all men'. It is a point of contention among historians whether Lodge wished, like the irreconcilables, to kill the League or merely to make it 'safe' for the United States. The evidence tilts slightly towards the latter. Nevertheless, Lodge was sceptical about the League of Nations from the outset and saw it as grievously flawed; he expressed the opinion privately that it was 'a mere ornament'. Real force would continue to lie with the great powers.

A Summary of Lodge Reservations Tabled in the Senate in November 1919

- Congress to have the right to immediate withdrawal from the League of Nations dependent upon the United States fulfilling her international obligations.
- A repudiation of Article 10. The United States should have no

obligation to employ military or naval forces unless in any
particular case Congress should so provide.

• The United States should refuse arbitration or inquiry by the
League of Nations Assembly or Council regarding any question
related to the Monroe Doctrine.

• Opposition to the Shantung Clauses of the Treaty of Versailles.

• An assertion of Congressional powers of appointment of League
of Nations representatives to the Assembly, Council, and
Commissions and over decision-making on contributions to the
expenses of the League of Nations.

• Congressional powers to increase armaments if it saw fit.

• The United States should not consider itself bound by League
decisions in which any member of the League and its self-
governing dominions had cast more than one vote.

The differences between Lodge and Wilson have been succinctly
summarised by one recent historian: 'Activism and leadership in
traditional power politics were what Lodge wanted for the United
States; activism and leadership in building an international structure of
peace and justice were what Wilson wanted for his country'. They
disagreed less about the desirability or extent of America's overseas
commitments than about the aims behind such commitments. Lodge
was quick to emphasise, however, that: 'There is a wide difference
between taking a suitable part and bearing due responsibility in world
affairs and plunging the United States into every controversy and
conflict on the face of the globe.' He wrote of Wilson's peacemaking:

1 He should have said to the powers associated with us in the war:
'We want the world made safe against Germany and as long as that
is done we are content. So far as European matters are concerned,
you are the people to settle them. Settle them all among yourselves
5 and we will back you up. When it comes to Asia and Africa, of
course we will expect to have a voice; and we ask to be left alone in
our own hemisphere'. If that had been done the situation today
would have been wholly different. But Mr. Wilson has undertaken
to be the final umpire in every European question, incurring
10 hostility both for himself and his country, and meddling with
things in which the United States has no interest whatsoever.

Article 10 threatened to involve the United States in a war that was not
of its choosing, a war that might take place far away without touching
vital American interests. Why should the American people assume the
risk of war to prevent a border dispute in the Balkans, maintain Japanese
control in the disputed Shantung Province, or uphold British rule in
Ireland and India?

Lodge was probably willing to acquiesce in ratification on the basis of strong and effective reservations. Strong reservationists accepted most of the provisions of the treaty unrelated to the League of Nations and were prepared to turn a blind eye to ones they disliked. They were also prepared to accept American membership of the League of Nations but insisted upon reserving to the United States, and specifically Congress, the power of decision as regards the extent of American participation. They rejected an open-ended binding promise to enforce collective security anywhere. Wilson never gave a convincing interpretation of the United States' responsibilities under Article 10. He preferred to ignore the paradox that in order to keep the peace it might be necessary to go to war. The League as depicted in Wilson's Fourteen Points address rested on the effectiveness of an implied threat to use force. It would be a League so morally ascendant that force would never actually have to be used. This was too vague for Lodge, who also refused to accept Wilson's attempt in August 1919 to distinguish between a moral and a legal obligation, an explanation which seemed like playing with words (Wilson described the article as 'binding in conscience only, not in law'). Those who emphasise Lodge's willingness to accept the treaty with reservations point to the fact that he allowed a second vote in February 1920 and had been prepared to enter a bipartisan conference in January 1920 to seek compromise language. Lodge was distrusted by the irreconcilables and praised by Viscount Grey, the British ambassador, who advocated British acceptance of the Lodge reservations as the best means of securing American participation in the League of Nations. It is impossible to measure public opinion on this question accurately, but the overwhelming majority of thoughtful people favoured ratification with some kind of reservations. They were not to get their wish. The treaty with Lodge reservations and supported by 21 Democrat Senators failed by seven votes to secure a two-thirds majority on 19 March 1920, defeated by an unlikely combination of Democrats loyal to Wilson and the irreconcilables.

6 Wilson and the Treaty Fight

The only hope for the treaty depended upon Wilson's acceptance of reservations, but Wilson held firmly to his vision of collective security and refused to accept a more limited but definite role for his country in international relations. His uncompromising position was clear in a letter written to Joe Tumulty in June 1919:

1 My clear conviction is that the adoption of the treaty by the Senate with reservations would put the United States as clearly out of the concert of nations as a rejection. We ought either to go in or stay out. To stay out would be fatal to the influence and even to the
5 commercial prospects of the United States.

In the following months, the President rejected all efforts to work out a compromise, whether offered by leaders of his own party, Republican mild reservationists in the Senate, or Republican leaders such as Lodge or Eliah Root. Democrats became increasingly restless but most felt they had little alternative but to support Wilson in his all or nothing stance. It seemed that the President almost perversely insisted upon losing the treaty fight by championing a covenant unacceptable to his domestic political opponents.

Believing that the American people would support him over the senators, Wilson undertook a tour of the country in September 1919, travelling over 8,000 miles in 22 days. He headed into the Mid-West, the heartland of isolationism, before campaigning further West through Nevada, Utah, Wyoming, and Colorado. He delivered 32 major addresses and 8 minor ones. By any account the tour was a valiant and impressive achievement and resulted in a string of fine speeches. He attempted to stir public opinion and had in mind as a precedent his active role in the Preparedness debates of three years earlier. The President sought to educate public opinion through reasoned argument. He also aimed to whip up public pressure on the Senate and was convinced that he could sense the underlying wishes of the people. He was certainly met by enthusiastic crowds and there were signs of an increasing rapport developing, but by this stage he was fighting a late and probably unavailing rearguard action. Most senators, because of their six year terms in office, were not immediately susceptible to the pressures of public opinion. Thus, even if Wilson did persuade large and enthusiastic crowds by his arguments and oratory the effects would be negligible. Having said this, his rhetoric still carries conviction even in printed form. His final speech in Pueblo, Colorado recalled mothers who had grabbed his hand, shed tears, and cried 'God bless you, Mr. President' - "They believe that their boys died for something that vastly transcends any of the immediate and palpable objectives of the war. They believe and rightly believe that their sons saved the liberty of the world.'

Wilson mounted a strong defence of the League of Nations in his speeches deploying a variety of arguments. He noted that he had succeeded in extracting concessions from the Allies after criticisms from congressional leaders in March 1919. The Monroe Doctrine had been safeguarded maintaining American freedom of action in the Western hemisphere. He rejected the idea that the League would interfere with domestic questions such as immigration and the notion that the British Empire would be able to outvote the United States on key questions. He underlined the positive social and economic benefits to the United States which would result from membership of the League. He stressed the covenant's provisions for the peaceful settlement of disputes and also pointed to disarmament provisions. He attempted to calm fears over the obligation of Article 10, noting that Congress had a power of veto anyway and that the employment of collective military force was unlikely. Nevertheless, he saw Article 10 as being at the heart of the covenant; all nations had a vital stake in the maintenance of peace and should act to prevent disruption 'at whatever cost of independent action'. At Cheyenne he outlined his specific objections to the Lodge reservation in respect of Article 10:

> 1 what this proposes is this: That we make no general promise, but leave the nations associated with us to guess in each instance what we were going to consider ourselves bound to do … It is as if you said, 'We will not join the League definitely, but we will join it
> 5 occasionally. We will not promise anything but from time to time we may co-operate. We will not assume any obligations …' This reservation proposes that we do not acknowledge any moral obligation in the matter; that we should stand off and say, 'We will see from time to time; consult us when you get into trouble, and
> 10 then we will have a debate, after two or three months we will tell you what we are going to do.' The thing is unworthy and ridiculous … it would change the entire meaning of the treaty and exempt the United States from all responsibility for the preservation of peace.

The President reminded his audience at San Francisco of the alternative old system of international relations:

> 1 What was the old system? That the strong had all the rights and need pay no attention to the rights of the weak; that if a powerful nation saw what it wanted, it had the right to go and take it; that the weak nations would cry out and cry out as they pleased and there
> 5 would be no hearkening ear anywhere to their rights.

For all his fine words, however, the key constituency at this time was the Senate and Wilson's speeches changed few minds there.

Of course, the severe stroke Wilson suffered on 2 October, 1918, made a difference to the treaty fight. It was not until the end of December that he could work at all and then only for five or ten minutes. The extent of his incapacity was kept secret - by rights he should have resigned immediately in favour of Vice-President Thomas R. Marshall. Not only was he physically enfeebled but, as a recent biographer puts it, he was 'psychologically crippled in ways no-one around him could diagnose with sufficient certainty to justify removing him from office'. The disease undoubtedly exaggerated his unfortunate personality traits and impaired his political judgement. The leading medical biographer of Wilson was convinced that had Wilson been in full health he would have found a formula to reconcile the differences between the Lodge reservations and his own interpretive resolutions (given Wilson's uncompromising statements before his collapse this may be wishful thinking). After his stroke Wilson appeared to live in a world of unreality. Early in January 1920 he ignored the advice of all of his closest advisers to compromise and inserted in his Jackson Day message to Democrats a rejection of any deal with League critics and a call for making the presidential election of 1920 'a great and solemn referendum' on the treaty. He even made plans to run again himself. As an expert in the American constitution and political system he should have known that there was no way of converting a presidential election into a referendum on a single issue. As it was, in a muted campaign, Warren Harding side-stepped the League issue and his candidacy was backed by 31 prominent pro-League Republicans. The landslide victory for the Republicans in the presidential election in November 1920 did not constitute a foreign policy referendum but it was an unmistakable rejection of Wilson.

7 Conclusion

When the guns on the Western Front fell silent on 11 November 1918 there had been 50 months of unprecedented slaughter and destruction. The dreadful human carnage bred a strong conviction, embodied by President Wilson, that the Paris settlement should be a peace to change attitudes and that the First World War should be 'the war to end all wars'. Yet the legacy of bitterness made a just peace unlikely. That the peacemakers failed in their efforts was hardly surprising. The statesmen at Paris were not free agents; public opinion hampered each of the 'Big Three' as they constantly looked over their shoulders to see what domestic critics and interest groups were saying. This contributed to the fact that the punitive impulses of the peacemakers prevailed. Germans of all political persuasions saw the treaty as a humiliating diktat, onerous in its heavy reparations demands, and a betrayal of Wilson's peace principles. Nevertheless, it is important to note that at the time the punishment of Germany was a popular measure. It was ironic that the people's peace hoped for by Wilson turned out to be very harsh. The statesmen also missed the point that peace has economic as well as military foundations - saddling Germany with huge reparations payments was storing up problems for the future. Having said this, it is right to underline the scale of the problems facing the peacemakers. Every boundary drawn created grievances somewhere. The Versailles settlement freed approximately three times as many people from nationally alien rule as it subjected to such rule which was no mean achievement. Perhaps no-one could have done better given the constraints under which the statesmen were operating. Ultimately, perhaps, failure at Paris occurred because of world forces too intractable for simple diplomatic solutions. The Treaty of Versailles was undermined in the 1920s and collapsed in the 1930s less because its detailed provisions were ill-conceived but because the victorious powers, including the United States, later lost the will to uphold it.

President Wilson believed that the United States had a special mandate for leadership at Paris because it was relatively disinterested. It had no territorial or other spoils in mind and no secret treaties to implement. It could dispassionately seek to found the peace on general principles of justice, freedom, and self-determination. The League of Nations covenant would be a vehicle for fulfilling an American mission to lead the 'Old World' away from its traditional war-producing practices. The United States had successfully created a federal system encompassing a vast continent and the President saw this as a model for world organisation. Finally, the United States represented a unique morality - Americans, he suggested, were the 'custodians of the spirit of righteousness, of the spirit of even-handed justice, of the spirit of hope which believes in the perfectibility of the law and the perfectibility of human life itself'. The sad irony of the treaty fight with the Senate was that in many ways the detailed design of the League did not matter. Wilson himself had observed that the League was an institution which would have to grow, develop, and change to meet the circumstances of the times. This has led one leading historian of the period to argue that 'the reservations the Republican senators wanted might not have made much difference to the covenant, even if the President had accepted all of them.'

Wilson's vision failed to secure acceptance either in Paris or at home. Possibly it was unrealistic. Certainly the President avoided confronting the idea that the League of Nations might need to use force. In his world of democracies, with their underlying harmony of interests, with states reduced in armaments to levels which would eliminate wars of conquest and imperialism, and with solemn oaths of guarantee backed up by public opinion, the problems of war and aggression would be resolved. Wilson's opponents in the Senate ridiculed his faith in other countries' commitment to his vision. In 1921 the Harding administration negotiated separate peace treaties with Germany, Austria, and Hungary that included the same terms laid down at Paris except for the League Covenant and the administrative machinery for enforcing the settlement. Also scrapped was the security pact with Britain and France to which Wilson had agreed at Paris. Wilson's award of the Nobel Peace Prize in December 1920 was a hollow triumph. The Senate, and presumably the American people, had indicated that they were not yet ready for a Wilsonian world order.

John Maynard Keynes's book *The Economic Consequences of the Peace* when it appeared in the United States in January 1920 enjoyed phenomenal sales. It was seized upon by Wilson's opponents as an excellent weapon in the fight then raging. It was quoted extensively in the Senate as evidence of the infamous deeds committed at Paris. But General Jan Smuts, the influential South African representative in Paris, later regretted the personal attacks made upon Wilson:

1 The truth is America wanted a reason for denying Wilson. The
world wanted a scapegoat ... There were a few pages about Wilson
in it which exactly suited the policies of America and the World's
mood.
5   When I encouraged Keynes to write that book, I knew his views
about the statesmen at Paris. But ... I did not expect him to turn
Wilson into a figure of fun. These few pages about Wilson in
Keynes's book made an Aunt Sally of the noblest - perhaps the
only noble figure - in the history of the war ... Wilson was already
10 going down in America. In their hearts the Americans wanted him
to go down: they wanted to evade the duties he imposed on them.
The book was absolutely to their purpose. It helped to finish
Wilson, and it strengthened the Americans against the League.'

***Making notes on** 'The USA and the Versailles Peace Settlement'*

Your notes need to enable you to assess the strengths and weaknesses of
Woodrow Wilson's diplomacy at the Paris peace conference and why
the Versailles settlement that was finally negotiated was unacceptable to
the majority of the American people.

The sub-headings of this chapter should enable you to organise your
notes conveniently. This is a topic where the subtle differences in
outlook between the various negotiating parties needs to be understood;
in other words the detail matters. On the other hand it is important that
you do not become so swamped with 'facts' that you lose sight of the
broader issues. You might experiment with making notes in a 'pattern'
form rather than in continuous prose. When you come to revise there is
nothing more dispiriting than pages of closely written A4 hand-written
notes where you have to spend a considerable time fathoming out the
main arguments because it is buried in the densely written text. Your
notes need to enable you 'to see the wood for the trees':
Now try constructing 'spray notes' (see below) on the following themes:
1   In what ways was Woodrow Wilson successful at Versailles?
2   In what ways did the American President fail to achieve his
     objectives?
3   Why did the American Congress reject the agreement negotiated at
     Paris?
You will need to flesh out these 'skeleton' notes with detail and
examples but your notes will have helped to highlight the main points.

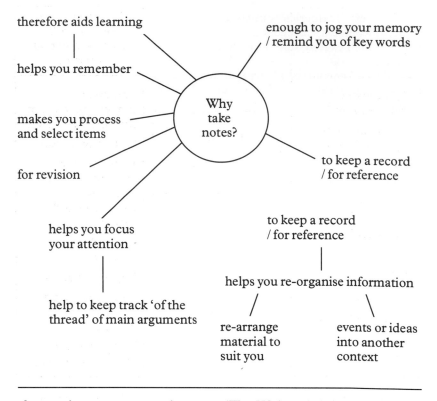

Answering essay questions on *'The USA and the Versailles Peace Settlement'*

Questions on this topic are most likely to ask you to make judgements on President Wilson's role in the peacemaking at Paris and his subsequent efforts at home to secure American membership of the League of Nations. The following questions are typical:

1   Should Woodrow Wilson be praised or blamed for his efforts at peacemaking from 1918 to 1920?
2   'He meant well - but he failed in every other respect'. Discuss this view of Woodrow Wilson's efforts at peacemaking from 1918 to 1920.

The text in this chapter provides you with plenty of ammunition with which to marshal a case either for or against Wilson. Plan an answer to one of the questions. You will need to consider some or all of the following issues: Why do the questions focus on the years 1918 to 1920 and not ask solely about the negotiations in 1919? What were Wilson's objectives and hopes in making his peace proposals? Were they realistic?

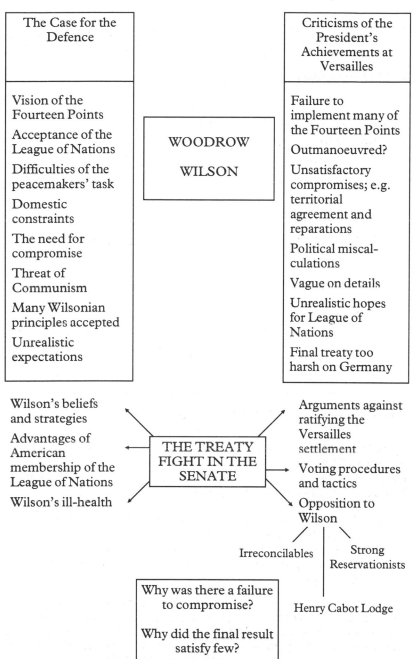

The Case for the Defence		Criticisms of the President's Achievements at Versailles
Vision of the Fourteen Points		Failure to implement many of the Fourteen Points
Acceptance of the League of Nations	WOODROW	Outmanoeuvred?
Difficulties of the peacemakers' task	WILSON	Unsatisfactory compromises; e.g. territorial agreement and reparations
Domestic constraints		
The need for compromise		Political miscalculations
Threat of Communism		Vague on details
Many Wilsonian principles accepted		Unrealistic hopes for League of Nations
Unrealistic expectations		Final treaty too harsh on Germany

Wilson's beliefs and strategies

Advantages of American membership of the League of Nations

Wilson's ill-health

THE TREATY FIGHT IN THE SENATE

Arguments against ratifying the Versailles settlement

Voting procedures and tactics

Opposition to Wilson

Irreconcilables

Strong Reservationists

Why was there a failure to compromise?

Why did the final result satisfy few?

Henry Cabot Lodge

Summary - The USA and the Versailles Peace Settlement

What were the constraints within which Wilson's peacemaking efforts had to operate? Who was Wilson directing his peacemaking efforts at? (Allied leaders, Germany, world public opinion, American public opinion, and congress all need to be considered.) If the American President deserves blame for his actions what were his main mistakes? Against what criteria should Wilson's 'failures' be judged? Whether you decide to come down for or against Wilson you will need to demonstrate an awareness of the alternative point of view. One tried and tested approach to questions like this is to outline briefly the case that you disagree with early in the essay. This then provides a useful 'Aunt Sally' target to attack in the remainder of your answer where you can state a vigorous counter-argument and explain the weaknesses of the case that you disagree with.

How should you start an essay question like this? It is important to write good introductions; first impressions count for a lot. There is no magic formula but the following represent useful guidelines of 'do's' and 'don'ts':

a) Above all you should address the question directly and explicitly right from the beginning of the essay. This does not mean repeating the question and your intention to answer it. You should put some thought into your opening sentences - they establish the tone and quality of what is to come in the body of your answer. Boring factual statements such as 'Woodrow Wilson arrived at Paris for the peace conference in January 1919' can have all the impact of a wet fish.

b) Relevant quotations or statistics which go immediately to the heart of the question can be very effective. There are assessments of the peacemaking efforts of the American President in the text made by Colonel Edward House, Henry Cabot Lodge, Robert Lansing, Jan Smuts, David Lloyd George, and John Maynard Keynes, as well as Wilson himself which you might find appropriate to offer as contrasting verdicts. Similarly, a contrast between the support of American public opinion for a League of Nations in 1918/19 as demonstrated by opinion polls, and the rejection of League of Nations membership in votes by Congress and the American people in 1920 also bears directly upon the question of perceptions of Wilson's peacemaking.

c) Your introduction should identify the main issues and areas of debate raised by the question. You need to establish that you understand the main 'point' or 'points' of a question. You should also 'introduce' the nature of the arguments to come which will form the themes of subsequent paragraphs. The key words in this particular case are clearly praise and blame, success and failure. It would be useful in your introduction to explain the basis upon which you intend to allocate credit and blame. What is the fairest way to assess the performance and decisions of politicians?

d) There is no optimum length for introductory paragraphs. One or two sentences is too little, a side of A4 paper is probably too much. It is the quality not the quantity that counts! Having said this, you might find it helpful to aim at a third to half a side of A4.

e) A weak introduction might contain some of the following features: unfocussed and unnecessary background waffle, a collection of facts which are presented without relating them to the question, or an immediate plunge into narrative without establishing the context and focus of the question. Don't waste ink unloading factual material or providing background which you think that you 'ought' to include. Imagine an examiner looking over your shoulder poised to write 'irrelevant' or 'narrative' in the margin of your work.

The final paragraph of your essay is also important. The most common weakness of conclusions is that they have run out of things to say and merely repeat what has been argued earlier in the essay. This will not gain you any additional credit. Try to keep one or two telling facts or details in reserve which will help to underline the arguments which you have presented in the middle paragraphs. Make sure that you do reach a verdict in your conclusion. You should be prepared to commit yourself. Sitting on the fence can lead not only to a sore posterior but an indecisive conclusion! Refer back to the original question and answer it as succinctly and clearly as you can. You might comment on the various interpretations or 'schools of thought' relevant to the issue in the title. One more mistake to avoid is to throw in a new idea that you only thought of as you came to the end of the essay. This will fit awkwardly with the flow of your argument. The conclusion should stem logically from the rest of the essay but have a fresh flavour which pulls the threads of earlier paragraphs together.

Source-based questions on 'The USA and the Versailles Peace Settlement'

1 The Versailles Settlement and the Fourteen Points
Examine the terms of the Treaty of Versailles (page 48) and President Wilson's Fourteen Points (page 41). Answer the following questions:
a)   Identify the terms of the Treaty of Versailles which might be seen as
      i) consistent with Wilson's principles ii) inconsistent with the
      Fourteen Points. (4 marks)
b)   What do the first five of Wilson's Fourteen Points tell us about his
      views on the causes of international conflict? (4 marks)
c)   How far is it possible to agree with Wilson's overall view of the
      Versailles Settlement that it was 'tolerably close to the lines laid
      down at the outset'? (5 marks)
d)   What did Clemenceau mean by his comment that 'Wilson talked like
      Jesus Christ but acted like Lloyd George'? How fair is this verdict? (7
      marks)

2 Contrasting views of the League of Nations and America's world role
Read carefully the extracts from speeches by Henry Cabot Lodge (page 59), and Woodrow Wilson (page 62), the Lodge Reservations (page 58), and the relevant text. Answer the following questions:
a) In what ways did Henry Cabot Lodge criticise Wilson's conception of America's role in the world? (5 marks)
b) What were the limits of Lodge's kind of internationalism? (4 marks)
c) How did President Wilson seek to defend the disputed Article 10 of the League of Nations covenant? How convincing do you find his interpretation of the United States responsibilities under Article 10? (7 marks)
d) Explain the statement 'the reservations the Republican senators wanted might not have made much difference to the covenant, even if the President had accepted all of them'. (4 marks)

3 Verdicts on President Wilson
Read carefully the extract from the writings of Jan Smuts (page 65) and consult the appropriate text in this chapter.
a) How did John Maynard Keynes make an 'Aunt Sally' of President Wilson? (4 marks)
b) What does Smuts mean by the phrase 'the world wanted a scapegoat'? (4 marks)
c) How did Wilson try to prevent America 'denying' him? (5 marks)
d) How far is it justifiable to claim that 'in their hearts the Americans wanted him to go down: they wanted to evade the duties he imposed on them'? (7 marks)

CHAPTER 4

The USA and Isolation, 1921-41

1 Introduction: The Basis of American Isolationism

In his Inaugural Presidential speech in March 1921 Warren Harding proclaimed:

1 The recorded progress of our Republic, materially and spiritually, in itself proves the wisdom of the inherited policy of non-involvement in Old World affairs. Confident of our ability to work out our own destiny, and jealously guarding our right to do so, we 5 seek no part in directing the destination of the Old World. We do not mean to be entangled. We will accept no responsibility except as our own conscience and judgement, in each instance, may determine.

In the Presidential election at the end of 1920 voters preferred to go back to the simple life exemplified by Harding's hometown of Marion, Ohio, rather than face up to the worldwide contention that America had been involved in under Wilson. The American public grew disillusioned by the outcome of a war that had not been, as President Wilson had predicted, a war to end all wars and to make the world safe for democracy. Every President from Harding to Franklin D. Roosevelt recognised the desire of most Americans to turn their energies inwards and the widespread belief that American intervention in the First World War had been a mistake. Reflecting this political atmosphere, the Senate rejected membership of the League of Nations whilst Wilson, its advocate, was in office. The Senate also refused to accept involvement with the World Court (more properly known as the Permanent Court of International Justice) even though it was proposed by Harding, Calvin Coolidge, Herbert Hoover, and Roosevelt. Between the end of the Great War in 1918 and the bombing of Pearl Harbor in 1941, the US Congress attempted to stay isolated from European affairs as much as possible.

It is relatively easy in hindsight to criticise American policies as an abdication of their responsibilities as a great power. In the 1930s it seemed that the United States was prepared to stand by as Nazi Germany and an expansionist Japanese regime sought to redefine the world order, even if such a redefinition was not to America's liking. Few Americans understood the complex relationship of the United States, the most powerful nation on earth, to the rest of the world. From the perspective of, for example, most cattle and wheat farmers on the great Plains or small businessmen, retailers, light goods manufacturers, and workers in service industries in the Mid-West there was precious little need for America to concern itself with events beyond its shores. One journal discovered that some Americans thought that the League of Nations was a baseball league. Elihu Root, President of the influential Washington-based Council on Foreign Relations wrote in September 1922, 'These plain people are our rulers, but they are untrained, uninformed and ... ignorant' folk who 'must become internationally minded'. This was important for the American economy because 'a large part of the influences which make for prosperity or disaster in our country consist of forces or movements which may arise anywhere in the world'.

In fact the American people remained resolutely nationally minded in the inter-war period. America's tough line on war debts and high protective tariffs to prevent foreign competitors gaining a foothold in its domestic market were examples of economic nationalism. Most European nations struggled to recover from the war in the 1920s. Much of the weakness of their economies was due to America's unwillingness to import European products and thus provide European countries with dollars so that they could pay off American loans. Public opinion was opposed to the cancellation or over-generous re-scheduling of war debts. During the brief post-war recession of 1919-21 it became obvious that the American people demanded repayment and that Congress would take a tough line. They supported the later view of President Coolidge who commented bluntly, 'They hired the money, didn't they?' Business nationalists and agricultural exporters not only blocked any attempt to lower tariffs but succeeded in raising them higher and higher, notably as a result of the Fordney-McCumber Tariff Act of 1922 and the Smoot-Hawley Tariff Act of 1930. This smacked of double standards - the American wanted 'Open Door' trade policies and equal access to all markets of the world whilst it shut foreign traders out of its huge domestic market. The self-serving and short-sighted policies of successive Republican administrations undermined global economic stability and prosperity.

After the stock market crash of October 1929 which preceded the Great Depression there was much international economic wreckage. For a long time the United States took no effective action to stem the decline in economic activity at home and lessen the impact on other countries. The London Economic Conference of June 1933 represented a last opportunity to co-ordinate foreign economic policies on debts, reparations, protectionism, and the management of currencies, but the United States failed to provide leadership and was represented by a divided delegation. Roosevelt's 'Bombshell Message' of 3 July 1933 undercut his own team of negotiators by ruling out any possibility of an international compromise: 'The sound internal economic system of a nation is a greater factor in its well being than the price of its currency in changing terms of other nations ... When the world works out concerted policies in the majority of nations to produce balanced budgets and living within their means, then we can properly discuss a better distribution of the world's gold and silver supply to act as a reserve base for national currencies.' America's position as a creditor nation at the end of the Great War should have given her every incentive to assume a role as international stabiliser in the Western world. In fact, although the United States was happy to enjoy the benefits of considerably expanded trade, there was no desire to take responsibility for the social and political implications of America's economic activity.

Nevertheless, it is important to recognise that there were principled considerations underpinning the isolationist impulse in American foreign policy between the wars. One leading historian of this period, Wayne Cole, reminds us that a policy of non-entanglement was 'the considered response to foreign and domestic developments of a large, responsible, and respectable segment of the American people'. Historically such policies seemed to have served America well. For more than 140 years after the Declaration of Independence in 1776 no US military forces fought in Europe. Expansion across the American West further developed a sense of American independence. A sense of escape from the corrupted 'Old World' reinforced isolationist sentiments and was touched upon in Harding's speech. Connected to this was the idea of America as an ethnic melting pot; as Senator William Borah, Chairman of the Senate Foreign Relations committee from 1925 to 1933, and a leading isolationist, put it in 1934:

1 This country has within her boundary people from almost every
   land under the sun, still conscious under certain conditions of the
   'mystic chords of memory'. Every civilisation has made its
   contribution to the American civilisation. How easy to transfer the
5 racial antipathies and political views and controversies of the Old
   World into our very midst. Once abandon our policy of aloofness
   from European controversies and we bring these European
   controversies into the American home and our national life.

The American Dream and sense of 'exceptionalism' was further reinforced by a fortress mentality, an assumption that the United States was an impregnable fortress protected by two giant moats (the Atlantic and Pacific oceans). Moreover, isolationists tenaciously defended American sovereignty and freedom of action. Opposed to collective security commitments, they wanted to leave Americans free to determine for themselves when, where, how, and whether, the United States should involve itself abroad.

Isolationists often gave domestic issues priority over foreign affairs - sometimes justifiably so. In President Coolidge's Inaugural Address in 1925 he said:

1 We have been and propose to be, more and more American. We

believe that we can best serve our own country and most
successfully discharge our obligations to humanity by continuing
to be openly and candidly, intensely and scrupulously, American.
5 If we have any heritage, it has been that. If we have any destiny, we
have found it in that direction.

If historians have found little to admire in Coolidge's provincialism and
resolute mediocrity, his conviction that the role of the United States
should be one of detachment from events in Europe and Asia was widely
shared. America became even more detached in the 1930s. From 1930
the effects of the Great Depression are difficult to underestimate; it was
the worst domestic disaster in the history of the United States, excluding
the Civil War. Confronted by widespread unemployment, lengthening
breadlines, and increasing poverty, it was understandable that the
American people and their leaders directed their entire energy to
domestic problems. During his 1932 Presidential election campaign
Roosevelt stressed a nationalistic approach to the problems arising from
the depression. He devoted only one very general sentence of his
Inaugural Speech to foreign affairs. Foreign affairs played no significant
role in the 1936 election. Many supporters of isolationist policies were
liberal reformers who believed that American involvement in a
European war would hinder the New Deal's attempts to bring about a
recovery from the depression. The America First Committee,
established in 1940 to oppose American entry into the Second World
War, sought, as its name suggests, to fix the minds of the American
people on domestic concerns. The internationalist Secretary of State in
the 1930s, Cordell Hull, admitted the sway of an inward-looking public
opinion over American foreign policy but claimed that attempts were
made to guide the people. In his memoirs, Hull argued that the
administration,

1 sought to keep reasonably ahead of public opinion, even while
seeking to educate public opinion to the importance of our position
in the world and to the fatal fallacy of isolating ourselves. But we
could not get too far ahead. To do so brought an inevitable
5 reaction and made the situation worse than before because it
caused the aggressor governments to believe that our people would
not follow us in any strong action in the foreign field.

Isolationist sentiment peaked in the mid 1930s with the Senate
investigations into the Munitions industry from 1934 to 1936 under
Gerald Nye, Senator for North Dakota, and the enactment of neutrality
laws in 1935, 1936, and 1937. From the perspective of the 1930s,
involvement in the First World War came to be viewed as a terrible
mistake. The Nye Committee persuaded hundreds of thousands of
Americans that an unholy alliance of bankers and arms manufacturers -

the notorious 'merchants of death' - had deliberately manoeuvred America into the war in 1917 for no more honourable motive than the desire for profits. Convinced that it was directly applying the lessons of history, Congress responded between 1935 and 1937 by passing a series of neutrality laws designed to prevent a repeat of the events of 1917. If war broke out anywhere, the United States could not trade with belligerents, send their ships into war zones, travel on belligerent ships, or lend money to those at war. Public opinion and an increasing number of signs of the approaching collapse of the European order led Congress to conclude that America must insulate itself. The Democratic National Platform in 1936, indicating the broad appeal of isolationist sentiment, promised: 'We shall continue to observe a true neutrality in the disputes of others ... to work for peace and to take the profits out of war; to guard against being drawn, by political commitments, international banking, or private trading, into any war which may develop anywhere.'

Cordell Hull recorded in his memoirs:

1 The Nye Committee aroused an isolationist sentiment that was to tie the hands of the Administration just at the very time our hands should have been free to place the weight of our influence in the scales where it would count. It tangled our relations with the very
5 nations whom we should have been morally supporting. It stirred the resentment of other nations with whom we had no quarrels. It confused the minds of our own people as to the real reasons that led us into the First World War. It showed the prospective aggressors in Europe and Asia that our public opinion was pulling
10 a cloak over its head and becoming nationally unconcerned with their designs and that therefore they could proceed with fuller confidence.

Many different groups of people supported isolationist policies. Not all, however, would have accepted the label 'isolationist' as this came to have emotional connotations and became a term of abuse. Supporters of isolationism were most numerous in the Mid-West and least numerous in the South. They were relatively stronger in the Republican than the Democratic party. Isolationist opinion was more pronounced in rural and small-town America than in the cities. In ethnic terms isolationists were relatively numerous among Irish, German, and Italian Americans. Yet there were exceptions to each of these generalisations; by the 1930s isolationism was a general American sentiment and not simply a Mid-Western phenomenon born of the insularity of the American interior. Moreover, isolationist legislators were elected in all sections of the country and represented both of the major parties. In Congress isolationist policies were supported by well organised Pacifist groups such as the Women's International League for Peace and Freedom and the national Council for the Prevention of War. Influential senators such as Nye, Borah (Idaho), George Norris (Nebraska), and Hiram Johnson (California) were powerful figures. Beyond Washington, the many newspapers owned by William Randolph Hearst warned consistently against entangling alliances whilst the isolationist radio addresses of Father Charles Coughlin based in Detroit had a wide audience. The anti-war movement was particularly strong on college campuses. Celebrated individuals such as the scientist Albert Einstein and the aviator Charles Lindbergh also provided influential support. These varied groups and individuals by no means shared the same views on many issues but they did broadly share a desire to preserve the American government's absolute control over foreign policy by avoiding long-term political commitments to other countries and to prevent involving the nation in wars overseas. The continued isolationist-pacifist attitude in the country was most graphically demonstrated in the agitation in 1938 for a constitutional amendment requiring a popular referendum on any declaration of war. The amendment, proposed by Congressmen Louis Ludlow, failed by only 21 votes, 209-188. Roosevelt had claimed that it 'would cripple any President in his conduct of our foreign policy'. Even an isolationist Senator was moved to protest that it 'would be as sensible to require a town meeting before permitting the fire department to put out the blaze'.

2 The Limits of Isolationism

In reality, America's relationship with the rest of the world was less isolationist in practice than the analysis to this point might suggest. Isolationism was as much a rhetorical as an actual cornerstone of American foreign relations between the wars. In other words, in practice America had many contacts and dealings in Europe, Asia and South America despite leaders emphasising the ways in which America was keeping her distance from 'entanglements'. President Wilson had proclaimed in 1919:

1 The isolation of the United States is at an end not because we chose to go into the politics of the world, but because by the sheer genius of this people and the growth of our power we have become a determining factor in the history of mankind and after you have
5 become a determining factor you cannot remain isolated, whether you want to or not.

Successive Presidents and Secretaries of State were unwilling to assume any political commitments in the international arena, to consider any proposals for collective security, or accept any limitations on America's freedom of action. Within this restricted context, however, the United States was involved in a wide spectrum of affairs; economic expansion, German reparations, naval and land disarmament, the creation of a new treaty system for the Far East (see page 106), many of the non-political activities of the League of Nations, and international efforts to promote peace. As Frank Costigliola, a leading historian of this period has put it, 'Americans sought involvement that was economic rather than political, unofficial rather than official, private rather than governmental'. 'Independent Internationalism' is a better description of American foreign relations between the wars than 'isolationism'. In other words, not retreating from the world (for that was impossible) but keeping American hands as free as possible to build a world order in which Americans could prosper.

The thinking and actions of Herbert Hoover, Secretary of Commerce from 1921 to 1929, and President from 1929 to 1933, in many ways embodied the idea of 'independent internationalism' (although his belief in protective tariffs, his distrust of Europe, and his support of immigration restriction demonstrated a nationalist streak). At the Versailles peace conference Hoover had served as director-general of economic relief; Keynes described him as 'the only man who emerged from the ordeal of Paris with an enhanced reputation'. He later became head of the American Relief Administration which aided famine victims in Eastern Europe and the Soviet Union in the early 1920s. Both Hoover and Charles Hughes, the Secretary of State from 1921 to 1927, believed it vital for America to increase its world trade. Together they developed a foreign policy that enabled the United States to continue to participate in the world's economic and political life whilst retaining a free hand in international relations. The Republicans encouraged private loans through big merchant banks such as J.P. Morgan as the main way of recycling cash for the purchase of more American exports; in 1924, for example, there was a loan of $110 million to Germany. Hoover devised a variety of strategies to tie private initiatives to public goals. For example, companies such as Firestone Rubber and Standard Oil were given monopolistic economic privileges in return for carrying out elements of American foreign policy in relation to the strategic acquisition of raw materials in South East Asia and the Middle East. President Harding described Hoover as the 'damnedest, smartest man I have ever met'. Hoover had the misfortune to become President as the Great Depression struck, thereby wrecking his political career. The American public believed that Republican administrations were following a policy of disengagement from international affairs yet the private sector was involving the United States in the intricate world system with the government's encouragement and making enormous profits from this economic activity.

Although the United States refused to join the League of Nations because of the political entanglements this implied, America was willingly entangled in world economic affairs. After the First World War, international economic conditions were overwhelmingly favourable to the expansion of American commerce. The war weakened the main European nations but America's manufacturing capacity was actually boosted by the war and US businesses captured many former European markets. In the 1920s, the United States flooded the world with products, assembly plants, and investment capital. The American Gross National Product increased from $128 million in 1921 to $204 million in 1929. Total US foreign trade jumped from $4.5 billion in 1913 to $10.2 billion in 1929. In November 1928 President Coolidge trumpeted America's 'foreign commerce unsurpassed in importance and foreign investments unsurpassed in amount'. American direct investment overseas in the 1920s increased from an estimated value of $3.8 billion to $7.5 billion. New York became the undisputed centre of the world's capital markets. During this period, Americans rapidly expanded their global dominance in mass communication industries - key new areas such as cable communications, radio, news services, motion pictures, and airline services. Efforts to assist Europe, Russia, and Japan in the early 1920s showed that Americans were beginning to understand how foreign aid could stimulate business ties as well as build diplomatic friendship.

Some historians have deployed the phrase 'dollar diplomacy' to describe American economic foreign policy in the early twentieth century. Definitions of the phrase vary. It might be regarded as the use by American business interests abroad of the political support of their government, support which they sought by every imaginable means. America thus sought trade and economic opportunity regardless of the chaos and revolution such a policy produced, for example, in Latin America. The United States then forced other nations to accept trade on terms favourable to itself and acted in an exploitative way. Dollar imperialism could be more positively defined as being a mutually beneficial relationship. The United States government sought to open under-developed countries to American capital and increase American capital already invested so that it could bring stability, prosperity, and political reform by using dollars rather than bullets. American foreign investment could contribute to world economic recovery and development ; for example, American investment played a useful role in bringing China, Mexico, and other countries into the global economy. Leaders such as Herbert Hoover and Charles Hughes believed that economic expansion would to some extent replace political and military involvement.

Alongside the influence of the dollar came the expansion of American cultural influences which could take many forms. In 1928 the National Geographic Society reported:

1 Travel where you will you can't escape American customs and fashions. Berlin flocks to its first elaborate soda fountain for nut sundaes, served by snappy soda 'jerkers'. American movies, automobiles, dental schools, typewriters, phonographs, and even

5 its prize fights lead in spreading American fashions and customs throughout the world. American automobiles have spread the gospel of mass production ... Typewriters have pioneered the way for a whole battalion of office equipment devices which have converted many people to doing business according to American 10 methods ...

This perspective was endorsed by the French ambassador to the United States in February 1930 who told Americans, 'Your movies and talkies have soaked the French mind in American life, methods, and manners. American gasoline and American ideas have circulated throughout France, bringing a new vision of power and a new tempo of life ... More and more we are following America'. In 1925 American films aimed at mass audiences comprised approximately 95 per cent of the total shown in Britain and Canada, 70 per cent n France, and 80 per cent in South America. These films acted as missionaries for American lifestyles and products. American voluntary organisations such as the YMCA and Rotary International, a businessmen's charitable association begun in Chicago in 1905, substantially increased their number of worldwide branches. In subtle but important ways this cultural influence and prestige (which declined with the onset of the Great Depression) enhanced the ability of the United States to conduct its political and economic policies in Europe with minimal cost and entanglement.

3 Relations with Europe 1921-33

At one level the 1920s were a decade of isolationist diplomacy as the United States maintained an arms length relationship with Europe (see the cartoon on page 80). Relations between Washington and the League of Nations, which was attempting to solve some of the political difficulties in Europe, were tenuous. The United States government failed for months to so much as open official mail from Geneva, headquarters of the League of Nations, in the early 1920s. Charles Hughes argued that: 'Helpful co-operation in the future will ... depend upon the fostering of firm friendships springing from an appreciation of community of ideals, interests, and purposes, and such friendships are more likely to be promoted by freedom of conference than by an effort to create hard and fast engagements.' Hughes and Republican inter-nationalists shared the opinion of isolationists concerning political relations with Europe. So did most Democrats and, for that matter, most Americans. They felt that European problems had European causes and should have European solutions. Thus, throughout the 1920s as France sought security guarantees against a future German attack, America consistently distanced itself from any specific plans. By 1930 France wanted a consultative pact with Britain and the United States as a price for reduced armaments. Both nations feared that a commitment to consultation with France would imply support if France were attacked. This was one of the rocks upon which the Geneva Disarmament conference of 1930-33 foundered.

Nevertheless, at another level America was actively involved in European affairs. As Frank Costigliola has written, 'economic imperatives, humanitarian instincts, and ideological impulses compelled American officials to take an active interest'. There was agreement between Republican policy-makers and American businessmen that the most important task of American foreign policy was to help rebuild European economies. Before the war Europe consumed over 60 per cent of American exports, including 83 per cent of all crude material exports, such as cotton, and 71 per cent of all foodstuffs. Giving aid to Europe was in America's self-interest. Until 1933, Republican

'I sympathise deeply with you, Madame, but I cannot associate with you',
5 December, 1923

administrations worked to rehabilitate Germany, relieve French anxieties by other means, advance disarmament proposals, resolve difficulties over war debts and reparations, stabilise European currencies, foster US exports, and encourage the flow of US capital abroad.

The interrelated problems of allied war debts and German reparations proved to be troublesome for relations between the United States and Europe throughout the 1920s. With the Americans asking for their money back, with France, Italy, and other countries refusing to pay off their debts until they had received reparation from Germany, and with the Germans declaring they could not possibly pay the amounts demanded of them, the scene was set for years of political wrangling. This widened the gap in political sympathies between Western Europe and a disgruntled United States. The French rechristened the United States 'Uncle Shylock' and cartoons in Paris newspapers changed the stars and stripes on the hat of 'Uncle Sam' to dollar signs. In 1922 the British Foreign Secretary, Arthur Balfour, accepted the French idea of linking debts and reparations - 'In no circumstances do we propose to ask more from our debtors than is necessary to pay our creditors'. Successive American Presidents, under pressure from Congress, refused to make this linkage. Congress passed a Debt Funding Bill in 1922 which called for repayment within 25 years and forbade the cancellation of any portion of the debts. Hughes went so far as to say that: 'The prosperity of the United States largely depends upon the economic settlements which may be made in Europe.' In general, American sympathies lay in moderate revision of the Versailles settlement. Reparations had been set at $33 billion by the Allied reparations Committee in April 1921. Germany was to pay $375 million annually from 1921 to 1929 and $900 million annually thereafter. In reparations conferences in 1924 and 1929 the unofficial American representatives, Charles Dawes and Owen Young, who dominated proceedings, helped to re-organise German reparations. The Young Plan of 1929 reduced reparations to about $9 billion to be paid over 59 years at an interest rate of 5.5 per cent. Moreover, despite French complaints, the indebtedness of countries like Britain, Italy, Belgium, and France to America was reduced by about 43 per cent in the 1920s as successive administrations moved from a rigid interpretation of repayment to a more flexible system which took into account ability to pay. Most of the arrangements proved to be academic once the Great Depression broke. A one year 'holiday' on German reparations and foreign debts owed to the United States was agreed in July 1931. Despite the Johnson Act passed by Congress in January 1934, which forbade private loans to any country that had defaulted on debts owed to the US government, every country except Finland did default after Hitler repudiated German debts.

The United States sought stability for Europe and pre-eminence without entanglements for itself. The 1928 Kellogg-Briand Pact, probably the best-known product of late 1920s diplomacy, symbolised this approach. Under an agreement sponsored by the American Secretary of State, Frank Kellogg, and the French Foreign Minister, Aristide Briand, signatories agreed to 'condemn recourse to war for the solution of international controversies, and renounce it as an instrument of national policy in their relations with one another'. If European nations did forsake war it would both underline the importance of America's economic superiority and ensure the security of its worldwide trading activities. Every sovereign state except three South American republics signed the pact. The Senate approved the pact by 85-1 in January 1929 which reflected the popularity of the agreement across the United States. President Coolidge assured a crowd in August 1928 that: 'Had an agreement of this kind been in existence in 1914, there is every reason to suppose that it would have saved the situation and delivered the world from all the misery which was inflicted by the Great War ... It holds a greater hope for peaceful relations than was ever before given to the world.' Robert Ferrell, the leading historian who has studied the Pact, has been rather less kind in his assessment: 'The Kellogg-Briand Treaty did not pretend to deal with the causes of war and did not suggest any machinery for settling international disputes by peaceful means. It simply outlawed war and placed an entire reliance upon moral compulsion for the observance of its provisions. It was the product of complete idealistic confusion.'

If official diplomatic links between America and Europe were insubstantial, economic and unofficial links, aided by the growth of American business and cultural influence in Europe, were considerable. Pre-war Europe had been the political and financial centre of the world. The impact of American culture after 1918 - the spread of Coca-Cola, Ford motorcars, and other elements of American civilisation - indicated the potency of the United States. The relative economic power of the United States was given a huge boost by the Great War as the table below indicates.

World Indices of Manufacturing Production, 1913-1925			
	1913	1920	1925
World	100	93.6	121.6
Europe	100	77.3	103.5
USSR	100	12.8	70.1
United States	100	122.2	148.0
Rest of World	100	109.5	138.1

These figures record the extent to which Europe (and especially the USSR) were hurt by the war, while other regions gained substantially. Naturally, it proved easier to develop and benefit from technological advances if one's economy was far from the disruption of the front line. Thus not only the United States, but also Canada, Australia, South Africa, India, and parts of South America, found their economies boosted by the industrial and food-stuffs demands of a Europe driven by a destructive war of attrition. According to one well-informed calculation, the United States' pre-1914 growth was such that it probably would have overtaken Europe in total output in the year 1925 if the war had not intervened. What the war did was accelerate the American advance and reduce the growth of manufacturing capacity of America's main European competitors who had barely recovered their pre-war position by 1925.

The United States had a domestic market so extensive that massive economies of scale could be practised by giant firms and distributors, especially in the booming motor industry. In 1929 the United States produced over 4.5 million motor vehicles compared with France's 211,000, Britain's 182,000, and Germany's 117,000. The chief New York Times reporter in Europe in the 1920s concluded that America's economic supremacy produced 'enormous political influence ... There is no country where the power of the dollar has not reached. There is no capital which does not take the United States into consideration at almost every turn ... Isolation is a myth. We are not isolated and cannot be isolated. The United States is ever present'. In fact this was only a partial truth. United States political influence in Europe and the rest of the world did not equate to her extraordinary industrial strength. Economic dominance did not necessarily translate into political clout. Whether one looks at critical issues like the efforts of Britain and the Europeans to achieve a system of security on the continent via the Locarno Treaty in 1925 or the work of the League of Nations in initiating arms limitation which began in 1926, efforts to shape the course of events to suit American interests via financial power were relatively weak. Moreover, a reluctance on the part of the Americans to do anything more than propose vague ideas like the Kellogg-Briand pact to aid European security, coupled with British, French, and Italian distaste over war debts issues, reduced American leverage with European powers.

4 The USA and Latin America Between the Wars

The American approach towards Latin America was far from isolationist. The Monroe Doctrine still served as the cornerstone of American policy. The United States sought to manage the affairs of the Western hemisphere and to bestow more orderly and predictable structures upon its relations with South American countries. In 1928 Charles Hughes proclaimed at a Pan-American conference, 'We do not wish to intervene in the affairs of any American Republic. We simply wish peace and order and stability and recognition of honest rights properly acquired so that this hemisphere may not only be the hemisphere of peace but the hemisphere of international justice.' The United States attempted to find means other than direct military intervention to continue its influence over Latin America. Primarily these means were economic. American-controlled businesses exercised significant influence in Latin American countries. The direct investment of US citizens jumped from $1.26 billion in 1914 to $3.52 billion in 1929. This investment was primarily in areas such as electrical power, railways, bananas, sugar, oil, and minerals. This was a third of the total US investment abroad and twice as much as Americans invested in any other geographical area. The goal of American control over Latin America remained but the methods changed. In 1933 Roosevelt outlined the 'Good Neighbour Policy' which had its roots in the policies of Republican administrations of the 1920s: 'I would dedicate this nation to the policy of the Good Neighbour - the neighbour who resolutely respects himself and, because he does so, respects the rights of others - the neighbour who respects his obligations and respects the sanctity of his agreements in and with a world of neighbours.' Things did not always look this benevolent from the perspective of Latin American countries.

It is true that after 1921 America began to retreat from the practice of direct military and political intervention and to accept, albeit haltingly, the principle of non-intervention, but in several countries the United States had a tarnished record. For example, Nicaragua was under US military occupation from 1912-25 and 1926-33, Haiti was governed by US marines from 1915-34, and the Dominican Republic was occupied from 1916-24. The self-determination principle was much abused in practice. The United States often acted on the premise that it knew what was best for its southern neighbours.

Wherever left-wing regimes threatened American business interests or the internal stability of individual countries the response favoured by Americans was to look for a strong man. For example, to put a stop to supposed communist infiltration in Nicaragua the Somoza family was supported after 1936. President Machado of Cuba conducted national affairs using a mixture of corruption and brutality from 1924-33 with the approval of American businessmen. State department representatives helped to abort a left-wing coup in 1933 and guided General Batista towards a position of power he was to hold until 1959. Another military dictator, Rafael Trujillo, was supported in the Dominican Republic after 1930. A self-interested rationale for American policies with regard to countries like these came in a remark Roosevelt is alleged to have made during a visit to Washington by Somoza; 'He may be a son-of-a-bitch, but he is our son-of-a-bitch.'

Undoubtedly Latin America was politically unstable. Between 1929 and 1931 revolution struck seven countries and by 1933 only Colombia, Uruguay, and Venezuela had escaped revolution. Occasionally

American mediation between countries could be a force for good. For example, under the Hoover administration the United States was quietly effective at resolving border disputes between Paraguay and Bolivia, and Peru and Colombia. However, American efforts to promote stability did not normally mean the export to Latin America of American liberal democratic values.

American capital and trade dominated in Latin America. The United States enjoyed special advantages in competing for markets at the expense of the older European imperial powers. Increasingly, the economic relationship between the United States and Latin America was mutually beneficial, but at times it was exploitative and produced cries of 'Yankee imperialism' (most notably in Mexico and Argentina). From 1918-29 exports to Latin America tripled in value and made up 20 per cent of all goods shipped abroad. American investment was often used to take over vital mineral resources such as Chile's copper and Venezuela's oil. Trade with Chile in nitrates and copper jumped after American investments there doubled from $200 million in 1920 to $400 million in 1928. American firms produced more than half of Venezuela's oil. In Cuba, American interests accounted for two-thirds of sugar production. Clearly there were considerable benefits from the scale of American investment - the traffic in goods between America and her southern neighbours was not one way as, for example, total US imports from Latin America increased from $1.2 million in 1914 to $4 billion in 1920. Equally, however, there were dangers in locking countries into risking one-crop or over-specialised economies subject to fluctuating world prices (which plummeted after 1929). Policy-makers sought to draw the economic relationship closer by the establishment of an Export-Import Bank in the 1930s. If a nation needed dollars it had to promise to buy US goods and reduce its own barriers to American investment. A Reciprocal Trade Act in 1934 reduced tariff barriers and helped to further boost trade. In 1935, for example, there were reciprocal agreements with Brazil, Colombia, and Honduras.

There was more to the Good Neighbour Policy than words. It was given practical expression. At a Pan-American conference in Uruguay in November 1933 Cordell Hull supported a resolution that 'No State has the right to intervene in the internal and external affairs of another'. The United States revoked the Platt Amendment of 1903 which had given it the right to intervene in Cuba for the maintenance of life, property, and individual liberty. The marines were pulled out of Haiti. A treaty with Panama in March 1936 abolished American rights to intervene unilaterally and gave Panama a joint responsibility for the defence and operation of the Canal. When Roosevelt attended an Inter-American Peace conference in November 1936 he was greeted in Rio by huge crowds lining the streets shouting 'Viva la democracia! Viva Roosevelt' whilst in Buenos Aires an estimated two million Argentines acclaimed the President and showered him with flowers. In Mexico in 1938

Roosevelt adopted a conciliatory line when the Mexican President expropriated the $400 million oil industry. Despite internal pressures to intervene from business interests and the State Department, a compromise deal was brokered by the American ambassador who advised his President, 'The Mexican situation will test our Good Neighbour Policy. The upholding of that policy, however, is of the highest consideration in a mad world where Pan-American solidarity may save democracy. Oil ought not to smear it.' There was indeed a turn towards greater continental solidarity in the late 1930s as Germany, Italy, and Japan attempted to improve their economic and political standing in Latin America. In the Declaration of Lima of December 1938 it was agreed that should the peace, security, or territorial integrity of any American Republic be threatened, American states would share a 'common concern' and would 'make effective their solidarity'. This agreement was fleshed out a year later with the endorsement of a 'neutrality zone' to ensure Western hemispheric security and joint efforts were made to cope with the commercial problem as raised by the outbreak of war in Europe. Roosevelt and Hull had changed Latin America's general mistrust of Washington to general co-operation by the time they went to war in December 1941.

5 FDR and Isolationism, 1933-8

One recent historian has written of Franklin Delano Roosevelt (FDR), 'Like a colossus he bestrode American diplomacy for twelve tumultuous years. Sphinx-like, he continues to baffle historians'. Pinning down the foreign policy principles of the skilful, charismatic, pragmatic, but opportunistic President is no easy task. During the first and most of the second administration of FDR the American people wanted to distance themselves from the realities of international relations. Because American efforts to support the League of Nations in stopping Japanese aggression and to encourage worldwide disarmament and economic co-operation had failed, public opinion, as well as official thinking, after 1933 was less willing to endorse a repetition of these efforts. FDR went with the tide of isolationist sentiment. Robert Dallek in his influential and largely sympathetic study *Franklin Roosevelt and American Foreign Policy 1932-1945* (1979) depicted Roosevelt as 'An American Internationalist' but entitled sections of his study covering the years 1933-8 'Farewell to Internationalism' and 'The Internationalist as Isolationist'. US foreign policy according to Secretary of State Hull could be summed up in the phrase 'keeping this country out of war'. This was the theme of a keynote speech made by Roosevelt at Chautauqua during his re-election campaign in August 1936 in which all of his rhetorical skills were evident:

1 I have seen war. I have seen war on land and sea. I have seen blood
   running from the wounded. I have seen men coughing out their
   gassed lungs. I have seen the dead in the mud. I have seen cities
   destroyed. I have seen 200 limping, exhausted men come out of
5 line - the survivors of a regiment of 1,000 that went forward 48
   hours before. I have seen children starving. I have seen the agony of
   mothers and wives. I hate war ... If war should break out again on
   another continent, let us not blink the fact that we would find in
   this country thousands of Americans who, seeking immediate
10 riches - fool's gold - would attempt to break down or avoid our
   neutrality. They would tell you - and, unfortunately, their views
   would get wide publicity - that if they could produce and ship this
   and that and the other article to belligerent nations, the
   unemployed of America would all find work ... It would be hard to
15 resist ... the clamour of that greed ... |But| if we face the choice of
   profits or peace, this nation will answer - this nation must answer-
   'We choose peace'.

The practical results of the popular and emotional instincts which
Roosevelt articulated in this speech were limited. A.J.P. Taylor likened
America's role in the 1930s to the episode when Sherlock Holmes
directed his friend's attention to the behaviour of the dog in the night.
'But the dog did nothing in the night', Dr Watson objected. 'Exactly',
Holmes replied, 'That was the significant episode'. Beyond vague
pronouncements of the need for collective action and expression of
peace and goodwill, the American government did very little.
   A strong case can be made in defence of Roosevelt's policies. It is
entirely understandable that his first priority was to restore confidence in
America's domestic economy. Leading isolationists in Congress were
largely representative of Progressive opinion within the Republican
Party. FDR needed their support in order to implement his New Deal
programmes. There are worse political crimes than bowing to
democratic pressure. Public opinion accounted for much in determining
the course of American foreign relations after 1933. Many historians
share Roosevelt's perspective that isolationist sentiment was too
powerful to combat in any direct way. The public outcry against
American participation in the World Court in January 1935, for
example, played upon anger over European countries defaulting on their
war debts and fears that Europe would draw the United States against its
interests into another war. FDR wrote to Henry Stimson,

1 In normal times the radio and other appeals by them would not
   have been effective. However, these are not normal times; people
   are jumpy and very ready to run after strange gods. This is so in
   every other country as well as our own. I fear common sense
5 dictates no new method for the time being.

A series of domestic problems later in the 1930s made it difficult for Roosevelt to risk a political fight over foreign affairs. There were setbacks and difficulties over his proposals to 'pack' the Supreme Court early in 1937, a severe economic recession in 1937-8, and Democratic reverses in Congressional elections. Moreover, FDR could point to the collapse of the League of Nations and the indecisiveness of US allies, for example over the application of economic sanctions against Italy after her invasion of Ethiopia. There was a distrust of British and French motives which had taken root at Versailles as both countries scrambled for imperial spoils from Germany. The British system of imperial preference established by the Ottawa Conference of 1932 was regarded with suspicion in Washington as a barrier to American exports. Roosevelt's private doubts about the neutrality legislation that increasingly sought to tie his hands were clear in a letter he wrote to Colonel House in September 1935. He complained of, 'the very large and perhaps increasing school of thought which holds that we can and should withdraw wholly within ourselves and cut off all but the most perfunctory relationships with other nations. They imagine that if the civilisation of Europe is about to destroy itself through internal strife, it might just as well go ahead and do it and that the United States can stand idly by.'

There is a case for arguing that Roosevelt was as internationalist as he could have been in the prevailing circumstances. Early in his administration Roosevelt gave diplomatic recognition to the Soviet Union and promoted the 'Good Neighbour Policy' in Latin America. A positive response to British suggestions for a combined policy in naval talks with Japan indicated a willingness to co-operate with other like-minded nations. He wrote to the American ambassador in Germany in August 1934, 'I too am downhearted but watch for any ray of hope or opening to give me an opportunity to lend a helping hand. There is nothing in sight at present'. He was stymied by events in Europe, domestic opinion, and the depression's resistance to New Deal recovery methods. Moreover, it is important to point out that international events were by no means always susceptible to American influence. Roosevelt was aware of the dangers inherent in German and Italian expansionism: he wrote to the American ambassador in Rome early in 1935, 'these are without doubt the most hair-trigger times the world has gone through in your lifetime or mine. I do not exclude June and July 1914'. The administration was internationalist in its trade and other policies. The reciprocal trade programme was a less nationalistic programme than that pursued by other countries in the 1930s (Nazi Germany and Fascist Italy, for example, pursued policies of economic self-sufficiency). Cordell Hull, in particular, was convinced that the key to world peace lay in the recovery of the world economy - 'The truth is universally recognised that trade between nations is the greatest peacemaker and civiliser within human experience.' A healthy economy would allow 'settlement among nations of any political questions'. Roosevelt was less convinced than this, writing to the Secretary of the Treasury at the end of 1938, 'these trade treaties are just too goddamned slow. The world is marching too fast. They're just too slow', but he did subscribe to the principle of Free Trade as a soothing balm in international relations. The United States was clearly more sympathetic to the democracies in Europe than the dictatorships which became increasingly apparent in the President's speeches (see page 92). FDR did perceive threats to American interests outside the Western hemisphere, for example in 1936 when Germany re-entered the Rhineland or in 1937 when Japan moved south of the Great Wall of China. He was rebuffed by Britain when he proposed a world conference in January 1938 to discuss the essential principles of international conduct, the best means of reducing armaments, and equality of economic opportunity for all peoples.

Critics would argue that Roosevelt could have done more than he did to combat isolationist sentiment, especially during his first term of office, and might have provided bolder presidential leadership. He did have a clear mandate; in 1936 his popular vote exceeded that of his Republican opponent, Alfred Landon, by 11 million. He did not attempt to educate the American public to the dangers of the international situation until at least 1937. Although he complained privately, he accepted the isolationist victories of 1935-7 with almost no public remonstration. His attempts to rouse American opinion through for example the Quarantine speech of August 1937 (see page 114) had only a limited effect and tended to strengthen British and French doubts about American reliability. FDR had difficulty living down his cavalier behaviour during the World Economic Conference of 1933. Neville Chamberlain wrote in March 1937, 'The greatest single contribution which the United States could make at the present moment to the preservation of world peace would be the amendment of the existing neutrality legislation. The legislation in its present form constitutes an indirect but potent encouragement to aggression'. American actions tended to be restricted to talking about ways in which the United States could influence others to keep the peace. Meetings such as the Brussels Conference of October 1937 which sought solutions to the conflict between China and Japan produced a lot of hot air. Peace plans for Europe such as that offered in January 1938 tended to be insufficiently thought through. Winston Churchill was later critical of Chamberlain's forsaking a 'last frail chance to save the world from tyranny otherwise than by war ... No event could have been more likely to stave off, or even prevent, war than the arrival of the United States in the circle of European hates and fears'. However, with French political instability and a German move against Austria likely at any moment, the American ambassador in Paris described a meeting of the powers, with America offering assistance as a mediator, as impractical and unrealistic - 'It would be as if in the palmiest days of Al Capone you had summoned a national conference of psychoanalysts to Washington to discuss the psychological causes of crime.' It is doubtful if the American proposal would have had any significant impact on the course of European affairs.

What Roosevelt tended to offer was gestures and a posture of helplessness as the world drifted towards war. FDR's cable to Hitler on 27 September 1938 was representative of the American position in world affairs; the American President hoped that war could still be avoided, urged the Munich powers to continue negotiations, but refused to assume any American responsibilities for any agreements that might emerge. Alarming international developments increasingly forced themselves upon the consciousness of the American people: the Ethiopian Crisis (October 1935), the re-occupation of the Rhineland (March 1936), the Spanish Civil War (1936-9), the Sino-Japanese conflict after 1937, the German takeover of Austria (March 1938), and the Czech Crisis of 1938. Through most of these events America remained a mute and detached observer. In some ways the passivity of American policies assisted expansionist countries. For example, trade records with Italy for 1934-5 showed a significant jump in the export of important raw materials; shipments of oil, refined copper, iron and steel scrap all more than doubled. American-German trade and investment rose throughout the 1930s. In 1937 20 of the top 100 American companies were involved in significant agreements with Nazi Germany, some of them with the backbone of the German military machine, the I.G. Farben Company. America's position as a passive by-stander was clearly evoked by a state department official writing in his diary in August 1939 shortly after the signing of the Nazi-Soviet pact which had shocked the world: 'These last two days have given me a feeling of sitting in a house where somebody is dying upstairs. There is relatively little to do and yet the suspense continues unabated'. FDR yielded centre-stage to isolationist sentiment in the 1930s. There were understandable reasons for doing this, but he might have put up more of a fight. In the longer term a policy that amounted to keeping out of trouble spots was not much of a policy.

6 The End of Isolationism

Increasingly, from early in 1939, Roosevelt took it upon himself to educate the public and Congress and convince them that American security would be threatened if aggressor nations prevailed. By 1939 the United States faced a dangerous world. Japan seemed well on the way to East Asian dominance whilst Hitler, having annexed Austria, prepared for the next victim. In January 1939, in his annual message to Congress, FDR focused on international developments in contrast to earlier priorities. He called for the United States to use all 'methods short of war, but stronger and more effective than mere words' to deter aggression. At about this time Roosevelt agreed to the French purchase of thousands of American aeroplanes. He announced a massive American re-armament programme which called for additional defence expenditure of over half a billion dollars. Shortly afterwards Roosevelt met members of the Senate Military Affairs Committee informing them that he did 'not belong to a school of thought that says we can draw a line of defence around this country and live completely and solely to ourselves'. He argued that if the Axis powers conquered Europe, Africa would automatically fall and that following on from this Central and South America would also be threatened. The President traced steps by which Hitler might conceivably bring individual Latin American countries under his control and noted that Hitler had little regard for the United States, seeing it as a 'mongrel society'. In April 1939, when Roosevelt sought assurances from Germany that 31 named countries would not be attacked for 10 years, his appeal was turned aside dismissively. In the spring and summer of 1939 Hitler considered America 'hopelessly weak' and incapable of interfering with his plans. The continuing strength of isolationist sentiment was evident in Roosevelt's failure in July 1939 to secure a revision of the neutrality act calling for an embargo on armaments to all belligerents whether attacked or attacker. Nevertheless, although isolationists fought a tenacious rearguard action between 1939 and 1941, their dominance slowly ebbed away. In his annual message to Congress in 1940 the President underlined the impossibility of continuing on an isolationist course - 'I hope that we shall have fewer American ostriches in our midst. It is not good for the ultimate health of ostriches to bury their heads in the sand.'

Following the outbreak of war in Europe in September 1939, Roosevelt was the consummate political tactician as he guided Congress and the American people along the paths that the United States was to pursue in foreign affairs during the next 27 months. In his Fireside Chat of 3 September 1939, unlike Woodrow Wilson before him, he did not call for neutrality in thought - 'even a neutral cannot be asked to close his mind or his conscience'. From the outset the President emphasised his determination to keep the nation out of war. At no time before the Japanese attack on Pearl Harbor on 7 December 1941 did a majority of the American people favour a declaration of war by the United States on the Axis states. In fact, during most of 1940 and 1941 about 80 per cent of American people opposed a declaration of war. Nevertheless, an increasingly large majority did favour extending aid-short-of-war to victims of Axis aggression. In November 1939 the administration succeeded in repealing the arms embargo. Britain and France now had access to American arms production, although they had to pay for and receive armaments in American ports and ship the goods themselves - the so-called 'cash and carry' provision. In 1940 Hitler's rapid conquest of France and the Low Countries, his siege of Britain, and alliance with Japan shredded America's sense of security. A very real possibility existed that America would find itself an island in a world dominated by the Axis powers. In an important speech at the University of Virginia in June 1940 Roosevelt made his 'great commitment' to Britain (against the advice of his principal advisers who doubted Britain's ability to resist and urged him to preserve all war materials for America's own defence):

1 Perception of danger, danger to our institutions, may come slowly
   or it may come with a rush and a shock as it has to the people of the
   United States in the past few months ... Some indeed still hold to
   the now obvious delusion that we of the United States can safely
5 permit the United States to become a lone island in a world
   dominated by the philosophy of force. Such an island may be the
   dream of those who still talk and vote as isolationists. Such an

Uncle Sam and Isolation from European Affairs

island represents to me and to the overwhelming majority of
Americans today a helpless nightmare ... the nightmare of a people
10 lodged in prison, handcuffed, hungry, and fed through the bars
from day to day by the contemptuous, unpitying masters of other
continents ... Let us not hesitate - all of us - to proclaim certain
truths. Overwhelmingly we, as a Nation - and this applies to all the
15 other American nations - are convinced that military and naval
victory for the gods of force and hate would endanger the
institutions of democracy in the western world, and that equally,
therefore, the whole of our sympathies lies with those nations that
are giving their lifeblood in combat against these forces.

Roosevelt extended aid to Britain in a series of steps. He developed a
strong rapport with the new British Prime Minister, Winston Churchill.
In May 1940 Churchill's 'shopping list', in his first official
communication with Roosevelt, requested 40-50 of America's older
destroyers to help combat the attacks of German submarines on British
convoys. By mid-August, with the Battle of Britain raging in the skies
over Britain, Churchill promised to fight on 'until in God's good time,
the New World, with all its power and might, steps forth to the rescue
and the liberation of the Old'. The American intervention was not as
clear-cut as this (Lord Halifax, the British ambassador in Washington,
complained that dealing with the Americans was 'like hitting wads of
cotton wool') but a Destroyers for Bases deal was agreed in September
1940 whereby American destroyers were swapped for leases on British
bases in the Western hemisphere. Also in September 1940 the President
signed the first peacetime selective service or conscription bill into law
requiring the registration of all male citizens aged 21-36. In a long letter
in December 1940 Churchill set out Britain's needs in detail and
admitted that the time was coming when Britain would 'no longer be
able to pay cash'. The President warned the American public that 'If
Great Britain goes down the Axis powers will control the continents of
Europe, Asia, Africa, Australasia, and the high seas - and they will be in a
position to bring enormous military and naval resources against this
hemisphere.' A victorious German navy would disrupt American trade.
A totalitarian Europe (and perhaps South America) would endanger
what was left of democratic government. Roosevelt presented the
Lend-Lease Plan to Congress in January 1941. He compared the plan to
lending one's garden hose to help a neighbour put out a fire in his home.
The plan was finally agreed in March 1941 and authorised the President
to 'sell, transfer title to, exchange, lease, lend, or otherwise dispose of'
any 'defence article' to 'the government of any country whose defence
the President deems vital to the defence of the United States'. It was
effectively a declaration of economic warfare against the Axis powers.
    Isolationists continued to oppose the President's actions charging
that Roosevelt's methods short-of-war were actually steps to war. The

America First Committee established in September 1940 proved to be a highly vocal isolationist mass pressure group, building up a total national membership of over 800,000. Major newspapers such as the *Chicago Tribune* and prominent individuals such as Charles Lindbergh charged that Europe's war was none of America's business and at every opportunity accused Roosevelt of a deliberate plot to plunge America into the conflict. They regarded Roosevelt's tactics as dishonest and evasive. In the Lend-Lease debate one senator replied to FDR's garden hose metaphor that lending military supplies was more like lending chewing gum - 'You don't want it back'. The historian Charles Beard argued that the Lend-Lease bill would be better entitled 'An Act to place all the wealth and all the men and women of the United States at the free disposal of the President, to permit him to transfer or carry goods to any foreign government he may be pleased to designate, anywhere in the world, to authorise him to wage undeclared war for anybody, anywhere in the world, until the affairs of the world are ordered to suit his policies ...'. Such complaints were in vain; the legislation passed by 60:31 in the Senate and 317:71 in the House of Representatives. The isolationist alliance of Republicans, Roosevelt haters, New Deal activists, Mid-West Progressives, and spokesmen of an earlier, simpler, safer America no longer represented the mainstream. Nevertheless, isolationists went down fighting and did not concede defeat before Pearl Harbor. As late as August 1941 the House of Representatives only extended the Selective Service Act by one vote - the slimness of the victory indicating the limits of interventionism.

As the United States became, in Roosevelt's words, 'the great arsenal of democracy', America edged towards an undeclared shooting war in the Atlantic in 1941. Roosevelt sought to ensure that American aid reached its intended destination and was not sunk by German submarines or bombers. Co-operation with Britain was further extended in 1941 with Anglo-American naval planning, American convoying of merchant ships, and an extension of US naval patrols far out into the Atlantic. The US navy occupied Greenland to build bases and other facilities. In July 1941 61 per cent of Americans approved of Roosevelt's public announcement of the sending of marines to Iceland to prevent a possible German invasion and use of the country as a base against the Western hemisphere. There is a case for arguing that the United States crossed the threshold from peace to war in July 1941, as the war widened in Europe, the Atlantic lifeline came under attack, the British sought more aid, public opinion became more interventionist, and armaments production pulled the United States out of depression. Roosevelt extended Lend-Lease aid to the Soviet Union following the German invasion of June 1941. At a famous conference at sea off Newfoundland in August 1941 Roosevelt and Churchill agreed upon more aid for Britain and a Europe-First policy. In other words priority would be given to the defeat of Germany in Europe even if Japan further extended the scope of her expansion in East Asia and America and Britain found themselves at war in the Pacific theatre. There was also a public declaration of liberal war aims in the Atlantic Charter that was the Second World War's equivalent of Wilson's Fourteen Points (although three quarters of Americans still opposed a declaration of war!). There was an increasing number of attacks on American shipping, although Germany tried to avoid shooting incidents. Nevertheless, in September 1941, following an attack on the US destroyer *Greer*, Roosevelt issued a shoot-on-sight policy - 'When you see a rattlesnake poised to strike, you do not wait until he has struck before you crush him ...'. Less than three weeks before Pearl Harbor Congress approved the arming of American merchant ships.

President Roosevelt's handling of American foreign policy from 1939 to 1941 attracted much criticism from isolationists. It is fair to say that he was less than open with the American people. Presenting his Lend-Lease idea Roosevelt claimed that it decreased the chances of American involvement in the war. He kept some of his actions hidden from scrutiny - for example, the secret talks between British and American planners in Washington. He equivocated over American aid to the Allies in the 'Battle of the Atlantic' and did not tell the people about America's unneutral acts (for example, American naval units pinpointed the location of German submarines which allied ships duly attacked). Campaigning for re-election in October 1940 against Wendell Willkie, a relatively progressive Republican, FDR promised American parents, 'Your boys are not going to be sent into any foreign wars.' Charles Lindbergh urged open discussion, more congressional authority in foreign affairs, and limitations on the President's war-making powers. In May 1941 he complained that the President asked Americans to fight for the 'Four Freedoms' (of speech and worship and from want and fear) but then denied them the freedom to vote on vital issues and freedom of information - the right of a free people to know where they are being led by their government. Others at the time of the Lend-Lease debate accused Roosevelt of assuming dictatorial powers or at least feared setting precedents that could lead to dictatorship at the hands of others. Roosevelt worked hard to destroy isolationism as a political force by any means possible, including less than honest ones. He depicted leading isolationists as narrow, self-serving, partisan, and possibly Nazi sympathisers. A campaign speech in November 1940 denounced 'certain voices within our own national community, composed of men who call themselves Americans but who would destroy America' (the FBI found no grounds to substantiate charges of direct Nazi sympathies within the America First organisation). Nevertheless, interventionists later considered that, given the Axis challenge abroad and the strength of the domestic isolationist opposition, the ends justified Roosevelt's means. If historians have criticised the indecisive nature of Roosevelt's foreign policies in the

1930s and an excessive concern for congressional and public opinion, on many occasions between 1939 and 1941 he demonstrated brave leadership (for example, going against the grain of opinion inside and outside his administration in agreeing Lend-Lease aid to the Soviet Union). His political skills in gradually extending the aid-short-of-war policy and in fashioning a bipartisan national consensus in an election year have also been admired by historians. This consensus was symbolised by Roosevelt's decision to appoint two prominent Republicans, Frank Knox and Henry Stimson, to serve as Secretaries of the Navy and Army respectively.

In December 1941, although isolationists had been highly critical of the President and his policies, and many believed that the administration had provoked Japan into attacking, they united behind the American government in opposition to Japan and Germany. Nevertheless, most leading isolationists continued to believe that their policies had been right before Pearl Harbor. The final statement of the America First Committee as it agreed to dissolve itself read, 'Our Principles were right. Had they been followed war could have been avoided'. On 11 December, after joining with other senators in voting for a declaration of war against Germany and Italy, Senator Vandenberg wrote in his diary:

1   'We 'asked for it' and 'we got it'. The interventionist says today - as
    the President virtually did in his address to the nation - 'See! This
    proves we were right and this war was sure to involve us.' The
    non-interventionist says (and I say) - 'See! We have insisted from
5   the beginning that this course would lead to war and it has done
    exactly that.' Perhaps in a sense we are both right ... I say that
    when, at long last, Germany turned upon us and declared war
    against her most aggressive enemy on earth, it is no contribution to
    'historical accuracy' (to put it mildly) for us to pretend to say that
10 this war has been 'THRUST UPON US' ... But if this war is worth
    fighting it is worth accepting for what it is - namely, a belligerent
    cause which we openly embraced long ago and in which we long
    since nominated ourselves as active participants. The 'thrusting'
    started two years ago when we repealed the Arms Embargo.'

Most historians would disagree with his final point and would emphasise the sincerity of Roosevelt's desire to keep America out of the war. The United States was, as the historian Robert Divine put it, 'the reluctant belligerent'. The President was prepared, however, to take whatever steps were necessary to prevent an Axis victory because he believed that such a victory would threaten the vital security interests of the United States. The American people were finally prepared to jettison their isolationist sentiments to fight for a just cause.

Making Notes on 'The USA and Isolation 1921-41'

There are a number of important themes addressed in this chapter. In the first instance your notes should enable you to answer the following questions:

1 Why did America seek to avoid foreign entanglements in the 1920s and 1930s? (Your notes on the previous chapter outlining why America failed to join the League of Nations will provide a starting point here)
2 Who made up the bulk of isolationist supporters?
3 What evidence exists of the strength of isolationist opinion in the 1930s?
4 Why did isolationist sentiment peak in the mid 1930s?

Take these four questions and try to construct your notes as an answer to them.

You should also have a framework upon which to base an evaluation of the limits and extent of American isolationism in this period. This requires a fleshing out of what the grand sounding phrase 'Independent Internationalism' actually meant in terms of the way that America conducted its foreign relations. Use the following headings to help you:

Trade expansion
The activities of American companies and banks
The expansion of American cultural influences
America's relationship with Europe in the 1920s
Efforts to resolve the German reparations problem
American involvement in international efforts to promote peace and disarmament (e.g. Washington Treaties, Kellogg-Briand Pact)
Active American intervention in Latin American affairs (make a note of four examples)

Your notes need to enable you to understand President Roosevelt's attitude towards isolationism and the extent to which, after about 1938, America was increasingly unable to distance itself from the realities of international relations. The following headings may be helpful:

Congressional pressures and constraints on Roosevelt throughout the 1930s
Economic problems within the United States
The failure of the League of Nations, Britain, or France to take a stand against German and Japanese aggression
Neutrality Legislation

Ask yourself whether Roosevelt could have done more to combat isolationist sentiment than he did. Make a list of possible criticisms of Roosevelt's leadership.

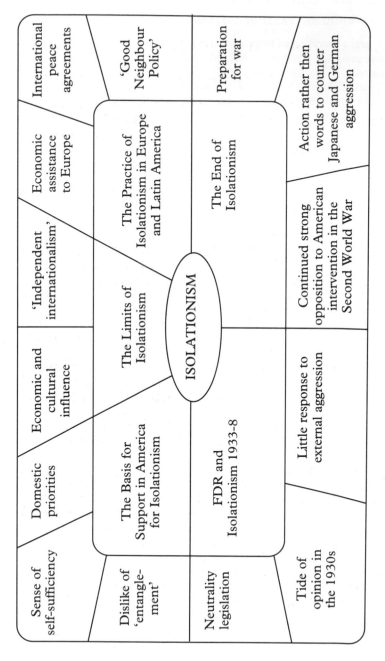

Summary – The USA and Isolation, 1921-41

Source-based questions on 'The USA and Isolation'

1 Two Views of the American relationship with Europe in the 1920s and 1930s
Study the two cartoons on pages 80 and 92 and answer the following questions:
a) Examine the first cartoon. Why would Secretary of State Hughes 'sympathise deeply' with Europe in 1923? (5 marks)
b) What might Hughes have meant when he said 'I cannot associate with you'? (5 marks)
c) Examine the second cartoon. What is 'Uncle Sam' referring to when he says 'It ain't what it used to be'? (5 marks)
d) How useful are these cartoons as evidence of contemporary opinion in America? (5 marks)

2 Isolationism in the Mid 1930s
Read the views of Secretary of State, Cordell Hull, on the investigations and findings of the Nye Committee of 1934-6 (pages 74 and 75)
a) Explain the meaning of Hull's statement that the Nye Committee 'confused the minds of our own people as to the real reasons that led us into the First World War'. (5 marks)
b) How far do you agree that American 'public opinion was pulling a cloak over its head' in its attitude towards the rest of the world in the mid 1930s? (9 marks)
c) 'Politicians' memoirs often demonstrate the wisdom of hindsight and are designed to place their authors in the best possible light'. To what extent does the extract support this generalisation? (6 marks)

3 Roosevelt's changing views on American intervention overseas
Read and compare the extracts from Roosevelt's election speech at Chautauqua in August 1936 (page 87) and his speech at the University of Virginia in June 1940 (pages 92-3).
a) What arguments does Roosevelt employ against American involvement in a future war in his Chautauqua speech? (5 marks)
b) Why did he choose to emphasise the theme of peace at this time? (5 marks)
c) Explain why there was a heightened 'perception of danger' in the United States by June 1940? (5 marks)
d) What practical evidence exists to support the view that American sympathies by June 1940 lay with 'those nations that are giving their lifeblood in combat' against 'the gods of force and hate'? (5 marks)

CHAPTER 5

The USA and Japan: The Road to Pearl Harbor

1 Introduction

The Japanese attack on Pearl Harbor on 7 December 1941 was one of the most dramatic events in world history. The Japanese launched two successive waves of attack involving 350 aircraft from a task force based around six aircraft carriers. The targets were the ships of the US Pacific Fleet anchored at their Hawaiian base. They succeeded in sinking, capsizing, or damaging in varying degrees a total of eighteen warships - eight battleships, three light cruisers, three destroyers, and four auxiliary craft. The US navy's air arm lost 87 aircraft of all types. Over 2,400 people were killed, listed as missing, or later died of wounds, including members of the army, navy, marine corps, and civilians. It is important to review American-Japanese relations in the 1920s and 1930s without giving the story the perspective of an inevitable war. Diplomatic efforts produced a host of genuine attempts to prevent confrontation. Nevertheless, an increasingly strained relationship finally snapped on 7 December 1941.

Pearl Harbor ended three decades of at best uneasy rivalry and at worst hostility between the United States and Japan. Woodrow Wilson believed firmly that Japan as 'the Prussia of the Far East' would be opposed to the West if it ever gained control of the Chinese mainland. America played a pivotal role in East Asia in the inter-war period - partly as a result of her considerable economic interests in the area but also because the United States was the only power capable of influencing the acrimonious quarrel between Japan and China. American fears rose as Japan built the region's most powerful military machine. Popular books appeared in the United States in the early 1920s with such subtitles as 'Must We Fight Japan?'. After 1922 the Republican Secretary of State Charles Evans Hughes was so successful in arranging a diplomatic solution for East Asia through the Washington agreements that he caused most journalists to abandon the idea that war with Japan was inevitable. Nevertheless, anti-Japanese feeling continued to be strong in the United States, especially in western states like California. A 1924 Immigration Law completely excluded Asians but was specifically aimed at Japanese immigrants. Joseph Grew, the American Ambassador in Tokyo warned in May 1933 that: 'The Japanese fighting forces consider the United States as their potential enemy ... because they think the United States is standing in the path of the nation's natural expansion.' By this stage Japan had occupied Manchuria, a north-east province of China, and left the League of Nations. Japan was committed to a policy of imperial expansion in the 1930s motivated by the combination of a loss of world markets following the economic crash of 1929, over-population, land shortage, and a need for raw materials such as coal and oil. Following the Japanese invasion of China in July 1937, the United States, under the Presidency of Franklin Delano Roosevelt, implemented increasingly tough policies directed against Japan including economic sanctions, a naval build-up, increased aid to China, and the deployment of the Pacific Fleet in a more offensive position. Unfortunately these measures produced not the desired retreat but the surprise attack upon Pearl Harbor.

2 American Interests in East Asia

When Theodore Roosevelt entered the White House in 1901 he proclaimed the Pacific an American lake and East Asia the nation's new frontier. America had annexed Hawaii, seized the Philippines, and proclaimed an 'Open Door' for China in the 1890s. His namesake and future President Franklin Delano Roosevelt argued in 1914 that: 'Our national defence must extend all over the Western hemisphere, must go out a thousand miles into the sea, must embrace the Philippines and over the seas wherever our commerce may be.' East Asia was perceived as an arena for the United States to use her wealth and power as she emerged as the world's leading nation after the First World War. Throughout the inter-war period the United States maintained a Pacific naval presence which aimed to hold Japan to a hands-off policy in China and, when this failed, after 1937 aimed to deter future territorial expansion. In reality, however, for all of their rhetoric, successive presidents accepted the primacy of Japanese interests in China. There were economic and practical constraints upon the extent to which America could flex her muscles in East Asia which the events of the 1930s were to highlight only too graphically. The Japanese Foreign Minister pointed out in 1924 that 'Japan, being closest to China, has an advantage by way of her transport costs and she also has the greatest competitive power because of her wages. It must therefore be a priority for Japan to maintain the great market of China'. American gunboats patrolled Chinese rivers, American troops maintained a presence on Chinese soil, and the Philippines remained a colony, but in the Pacific the Japanese were far superior. American leaders could lecture but not enforce. Nevertheless, they were unprepared to repudiate the hardy and popular notion that the United States should serve as China's protector and that China constituted an important commercial market.

America's main concerns in East Asia between the wars were commercial. A number of historians argue that the struggle for markets in Asia and elsewhere drove United States foreign policy in the late nineteenth and early twentieth centuries. If the United States could dominate in Asia, the largest and cheapest of all markets, she would consolidate her position as the World's leading economic power. In

1899 John Hay, the Secretary of State, issued the first set of 'Open Door notes' asking that the powers not violate existing interests inside leased territories that they acquired and that they not discriminate against other nations in setting port and railway rates. At this time threats seemed to endanger the American Open Door to China. Britain and Russia agreed spheres of influence in China for railway monopolies in April 1898 whilst Tsar Nicholas II of Russia and Wilhelm II of Germany wanted to close off parts of Asia's markets. At the same time Britain and Japan were colonising and cordoning off large parts of a fragmenting China. Successive Presidents in the inter-war period were committed to keeping the international arena open for individual enterprise; 'special privileges' (such as the growth of European colonial empires in Asia) were not to be allowed. The Americans secured a Japanese commitment denying any monopoly intentions in the Lansing-Ishii agreement of 1917. The Nine Power Treaty of 1922 enshrined Open Door principles in international law.

'Dollar Diplomacy' was practised successfully in the 1920s with both China and Japan. Trade with China was worth $190 million by 1930 and the United States had $155 million invested in China in commodities such as the utilities and telephone systems. Although this amounted to less than 5 per cent of total American foreign investment in 1930, future profits seemed limitless. A popular book title suggested that the Chinese should be seen as 'Four Hundred Million Customers'. In the 1920s the Japanese also relied heavily on the dollar economically. By 1926 Japan had borrowed $200 million and nearly 40 per cent of foreign loans were in American hands. American funds to Japan were instrumental in enabling the country to recover from the devastating earthquake of 1923 which destroyed much of Tokyo. Japan bought more goods from the United States than from any other country. In turn, America bought more than 40 per cent of Japan's exports in the 1920s. In particular, the United States was the chief market for Japan's large silk industry.

Allied to her economic interests America also had significant moral, humanitarian, and ideological reasons for maintaining a strong presence in East Asia. Again a self-confident sense of 'exceptionalism' was apparent; in other words America's relationship with other countries was perceived as different to that of other major powers. It was thought to have a higher moral purpose and was seen as lacking the exploitative elements of colonialism. Charles Evans Hughes believed Americans must seek 'to establish a Pax Americana maintained not by arms but by mutual respect and good will and the tranquillising processes of reason'. The United States did not want to join the European and Japanese quest for landed colonial empire; they wanted only scattered, relatively small areas of land to serve as bases for commercial expansion. President Wilson emphasised the moral service that would gently help the under-developed nations and refine the American spirit. In particular, he argued that the United States had a duty 'to play a part, and a leading part at that, in the opening and transformation of the East'. By 1920 there were 3,000 missionaries in China and by 1926 it was estimated that religious and philanthropic groups had invested $69.3 million in the country. In the 1930s FDR also expected great things from the twin forces of democracy and Christianity. There were three times as many American missionaries in China as Japan in the 1930s and three times as much investment in schools and churches. America sought to create through well-meaning paternalism and non military means a world characterised by legal, orderly processes and stability.

It is also important to recognise that the United States had strategic reasons to maintain an interest in East Asia - in particular a desire to limit the spread of communism. President Hoover commented to his cabinet in 1931 that Tokyo faced danger from 'a Bolshevist Russia to the north and a possible Bolshevist China' on the flank. The Soviet Union was committed to engage in anti-capitalist activities through the communist parties of other countries and through nationalist movements. America supported an unsuccessful mission by Japanese troops into Siberia in 1919-20 which had attempted to support 'White' (anti-communist) forces during the Russian civil war. In 1930 Hoover agreed with a journalist friend who wrote 'I think the Japs are our first line of defence in the Far East; and I am certainly glad they are well armed'. The Soviet Union was not officially recognised by the United States until 1933. It was certainly well within Soviet Russia's capacity to absorb neighbouring Korea. China, sunk in political chaos for much of the inter-war period, was a vast power vacuum into which Soviet leaders were presumed ready to move as soon as opportunity beckoned. The Soviet Union successfully established ties to various centres of power in China in the 1920s - the government in Beijing, various warlords, the Guomindang (the ruling body of the Chinese Nationalist movement), and the small Chinese communist party. For pragmatic reasons the leaders of the Guomindang, Sun Yat Sen, and after 1925 his successor, Jiang Jieshi, accepted Russian advisers, money, and arms. Jiang went to Moscow for training and every Chinese military division in the new national army acquired a Soviet adviser. In the mid 1920s Nationalists and Communists joined forces to launch a large-scale anti-imperialist campaign. They attacked American personnel and property in China and forced an evacuation of many foreign merchants and missionaries from the interior of the country. The alliance did not last long, and in 1926-7 Jiang began a long campaign to suppress the Communists. Nevertheless, following a series of bloody campaigns and the notorious 'Long March', a Communist Republic under Mao Ze Dong survived in the North-West province of Xensi. American aid sustained Jiang during the Chinese Civil War which lasted until 1937. The United States and Japan shared a fear of communism and Soviet Russia. This fear was to motivate Japan to join the Anti-Comintern Pact with Germany in 1936.

Clearly both America and Japan had to come to terms with the rise of Chinese nationalism in this period. Through the nineteenth century China had been ruled by the corrupt and ineffectual governments of the Manchu Emperors, who had never been able to exert their authority through the vast country. Finally the Chinese overthrew the Manchus in the revolution of 1911-12 and sought to establish a Republic. Policy makers in Washington usually disapproved of revolutions but in this case many Americans came to see China as a 'sister Republic'. President Wilson spoke of an obligation to encourage 'the liberty for which they have so long been yearning and preparing themselves'. However, the overthrow of the Manchus destroyed China's political unity for 15 years and there was violent disorder. Central government was unable to control provincial military governors and land-grabbing warlords. Rival power centres were established in Beijing, led by the official military regime, and Canton where the Nationalists established a base. In the United States there was a general sympathy for nationalist aspirations but a desire to maintain America's special economic interests whilst China was still in turmoil. Japan sought to take advantage of the confusion and in 1915 issued her Twenty One Demands on China which would have effectively turned China into Japan's protectorate. The United States and the rest of the international community successfully resisted these demands and the Nine Power Treaty of 1922, in addition to establishing 'Open Door' principles also bound the signatories, including Japan, to respect China's sovereignty, independence, and 'administrative integrity'.

Nevertheless, as Chinese nationalism surged in the 1920s, Americans found it increasingly difficult to pose as protectors because the Chinese no longer wanted protection. They were faced by a Chinese determination to gain control of their own country. The Nationalists under Jiang Jieshi captured Beijing and established their government at Nanjing in October 1928. The Americans recognised the regime as the legitimate government and a new trade agreement restored tariff autonomy to the Chinese. Americans warmed to Jiang in the 1930s and provided him with a variety of aid. He had joined the crusade against communism and announced his conversion to Christianity. His second wife, Meiling Soong, the daughter of an American-educated Chinese businessman, captivated influential circles in Washington with her beauty and flawless spoken English. Jiang encouraged Chinese people to move to the north-east province of Manchuria and sought to build a railway to compete with the Japanese owned South Manchurian railway company. He also encouraged a Chinese boycott of Japanese products. In July 1937 the Japanese attack on China was the direct result of newly aroused Chinese nationalism and the Japanese army seeking to preserve and extend its influence in the north of China.

The Manchurian crisis after 1931 (see page 108) exemplified America's other central concern in the inter-war period in East Asia.

This was a desire to avoid war. President Hoover articulated this
concern bluntly and clearly to his cabinet:

1 Neither our obligations to China, nor our own interest, nor our
   dignity require us to go to war over these questions. These acts do
   not imperil the freedom of the American people, the economic or
   moral future of our people. I do not propose ever to sacrifice
5 American life for anything short of this. If that were not reason
   enough, to go to war means a long struggle at a time when
   civilisation is already weak enough ... [Co-operation with the
   League over conciliation] is the limit. We will not go along on war
   or any of the sanctions, either economic or military, for those are
10 the roads to war.

Given the strength of domestic opinion opposed to foreign entangle-
ments, the economic problems at home, the timid policies of the
European powers, and the difficulties in taking unilateral action,
Hoover's position was understandable. American foreign policy in East
Asia thus relied mainly on moral exhortation and lecturing with little
practical follow through. It was a paradox also faced by Britain and
France in Europe that in order to keep the peace it might be necessary to
take military action. Yet America was determined to avoid war in the
Pacific. Thus, although President Roosevelt bluntly told Japanese
diplomats in 1937 that their attack on China violated 'the fundamental
principle of peace and order' he was unprepared to act. After September
1939 Roosevelt took the view that a conflict with Japan would reduce
the capacity of Anglo-American power to defeat Hitler's Germany. As
late as 1940 Secretary of State Cordell Hull sought accommodation with
Japan. He asked his Far Eastern experts 'to take a fine tooth-comb and a
microscope and go back over our relations with Japan and see if it is
humanly possible to find something with which to approach them and
prevail upon them not to gallop off on a wild horse'.

3 The Washington Years, 1919-31

The 12 years from the Versailles peace conference to the Manchurian incident were a relatively stable period in the relationship
between America and Japan. Within the framework of the Washington treaties, Secretary of State Hughes persuaded moderate
Japanese leaders that the United States and Japan would be better
off in a mutual co-operation arrangement. Japanese foreign policy in
the 1920s was usually associated with the name of Shidehara
Kijuro, Foreign Minister from 1924-7 and from July 1929 to
December 1931. Whilst Japanese ambassador to the United States
he had attended the Washington Conference in 1921-2 and was
admired by Americans for being temperate and conciliatory. A note

in 1924 illustrated Shidehara's general outlook:

1 In our restricted islands we suffer from a population increase of
700,000-800,000 annually. There is therefore, no alternative but
to proceed with our industrialisation. It follows from this that it is
essential to secure overseas markets and this can be done by
5 adopting an economic diplomacy. If we try to cure our economic
problems by territorial expansion, we will merely destroy
international co-operation.

As dollars flowed into the country during this period, Japanese cultural
life became more and more Americanised. The Japanese people flocked
to Charlie Chaplin movies and to dance halls. American films were
shown in even small rural communities, English words were
incorporated into the Japanese language, jazz bands were organised, and
the birth of radio broadcasting instantly transformed baseball into a
popular pastime. American fashions so influenced life in Japan that one
observer noted in 1929 'there is no part of Japan that has not been
Americanised'.

Much of the heat was taken out of the American-Japanese
relationship by the Washington agreements of 1922. The achievements
of these were considerable: the elimination of a naval arms race which
would threaten United States interests in the Pacific, a formal
acceptance by the powers of the Open Door in China; and an end to the
Anglo-Japanese alliance of 1902 which was replaced by a Four Power
Treaty. This stated that the signatories (America, Japan, Britain, and
France) would respect each other's Pacific territories. Secretary of State
Hughes had made a dramatic proposal at the opening session of the
conference on 12 November 1921. This was that the three major naval
powers scrap their capital ship constructions programmes (underway or
planned), build no capital ships for 10 years, and agree to a naval ratio of
5:5:3 (America, Britain, Japan) in capital ship tonnage. Capital vessels
were defined as warships of more than 10,000 tons displacement or
carrying guns larger than eight inches in diameter. One commentator
wrote that 'Hughes sank in thirty-five minutes more ships than all the
admirals of the world have sunk in a cycle of centuries.' With some
reluctance Japanese negotiators accepted a tonnage ratio inferior to
Britain and America, but in return secured a promise that America and
Britain would agree to freeze the fortification of their Pacific holdings
(the Philippines and Guam in America's case) at existing levels. The
agreement suited domestic purposes since none of the parties welcomed
the spiralling costs of a naval arms race. In other agreements Japan
agreed to return political control of the Chinese province of Shandong
to China and also consented to withdraw her troops from Siberia. The
outcome of the conference relieved some of the acute tensions which
had existed between Japan and the United States. There was an

awareness among Japanese that America had disliked many of Japan's past actions and had been suspicious of her future intentions. Nevertheless, the Washington treaties were perceived by many in Japan as a defeat. The British ambassador reported in November 1922 'the growth of feeling [in Japan] that at and since the Washington Conference Japan had yielded everything and gained nothing'. Sections of the Japanese armed forces - in particular the Naval General Staff and the Kwantung army in Manchuria - were increasingly prepared to question the foreign policy dictates of the civilian administration. An ominous feature at Washington was the attitude of Vice Admiral Kato Kanji; on the day Japan accepted the 60 per cent ratio he was seen shouting, with tears of bitterness in his eyes, 'As far as I am concerned, war with America starts now. We'll get our revenge over this, by God!'

Japan set about compensating herself for the restrictions in her battleship building by announcing increases in her cruiser, destroyer, and submarine strength. Kato was obsessed with achieving a 70 per cent ratio for Japanese safety, and as Navy Minister fought the London Naval Treaty of 1930 tooth and nail because it narrowly failed to agree to this level of strength. After some bitter in-fighting, the London Treaty proved to be the last success for those in pre-war Japan who put their faith in an international order regulated by the industrialised, democratic powers. To many Japanese, the Nation's salvation lay in its identity as an Asian nation not in compromising with Western countries. The Immigration Bill passed by the US Congress in 1924 was viewed by many Japanese as bitter proof of an American attitude of superiority and disdain. Many supported a more aggressive foreign policy to secure supplies of key raw materials. A member of the Japanese General Staff reflected a considerable body of opinion when he interpreted Japanese policy in 1923 as being to 'substitute economic conquest for military invasions, financial influence for military control and achieve our goals under the slogans of co-prosperity and co-existence'. Competition in economic life had the potential to spill over into military confrontation.

The problematic relationship between Japan and China - in which America was the main mediator - was shelved rather than resolved in the 1920s. The Washington treaties were a bold effort to help construct a new international order in East Asia, but the United States underestimated the strength of Chinese nationalism. China, torn by factionalism and civil war, was a loser at the conference. It was represented by the feeble Beijing regime rather than Sun Yat Sen's Guomindang government in Canton. America's Chinese policies in the 1920s have been defended - one expert, for example, praises the policies of the Coolidge administration from 1925 to 1928 which she says actively sought to help China achieve national sovereignty. Others contend that in the 1920s the United States missed an ideal opportunity to help shape the future course of Chinese national development. What is clear is that until 1928 the United States instinctively clung to its privileges such as favourable tariff rates. Meanwhile, Japan followed a responsible and conciliatory approach to China for most of the 1920s. Shidehara pursued a policy of strict non-involvement even when Japanese lives were at risk during the Chinese civil war. He focused on building up trade links - and about 25 per cent of Japan's total exports went to China. Hughes believed that he had built the necessary base for a joint United States/Japanese effort to develop China, but that the foundations he had established were not built upon. Chinese nationalists continued to be bitter that the signatories to the Washington treaties had implicitly given Japan control over much of Manchuria.

4 The Manchurian Crisis

The relative stability of the 1920s was abruptly shattered by the Mukden incident of 1931 - the beginning of outright Japanese aggression in China. On the evening of 18 September 1931 Japan announced that a group of Chinese soldiers had exploded a bomb on the South Manchurian Railway a few miles north of Mukden. The Japanese army quickly began to occupy the line of the railway and then gradually spread out into the remainder of Manchuria. In fact the incident was fabricated by young Japanese officers of the Kwantung army.

They had plotted for months to seize Manchuria and sever it permanently from China. Eager to expand Japanese power throughout Asia, they or their followers had already in 1930 assassinated the Japanese premier. The civilian government in Japan sanctioned the actions of the Japanese army after the event. The Manchurian crisis came to exemplify the failure of collective security in the inter-war period. It highlighted the failure of the League of Nations to cope with the emergency, whilst for the United States it demonstrated the inadequacy of the Washington treaties and the Kellogg-Briand pact of 1928 (see page 82). Secretary of State Stimson noted in his diary in October 1931, 'the whole world looks on to see whether the treaties are good for anything or not, and if we lie down and treat them like scraps of paper nothing will happen, and in the future the peace movement will receive a blow that it will not recover from for a long time'.

American national interests were only indirectly affected by the fate of Manchuria. Although the territory was ethnically Chinese, Manchuria had never been a fully integrated part of China (see the map on page 117). The United States officially recognised Japan's special interests in the areas of China that were closest to it. The Lansing-Ishii agreement of November 1917 noted that 'territorial propinquity creates special relations between countries and consequently the Government of the United States recognises that Japan has special interest in China, particularly in the part to which her possessions are contiguous'. In the Nine-Power Agreement of 1922 Japanese delegates did not seek specific exemption for the Japanese position in Manchuria believing it was already well recognised by other powers. The American Secretary of State skirted the issue but it was clear that Manchuria was a vital Japanese interest. The area served as a buffer against communist Russia (and by 1931 Outer Mongolia was sovietized). It was also the only place in the world available for emigration from Japan at a time when the census registered a population increase of 30 million in 30 years. Manchuria was also an essential source of raw materials such as coal, iron, timber, and soyabeans which were desperately needed by the import-hungry Japanese islands. More than half of Japan's foreign investments were in Manchuria. The Japanese-run South Manchurian railway was a nerve centre of these major economic holdings. By treaty Japan had acquired the right to station troops along the railway. In fact, Manchuria was more closely linked with Tokyo than with Beijing. Thus the issues surrounding the Manchurian crisis were not as clear-cut as the way China represented them to the League of Nations, which was as an invasion of an integral part of its territory. Nevertheless, the crisis demonstrated to the United States the inadequacy of the Washington treaties and the Kellogg-Briand Pact of 1928 which outlawed war as an instrument of foreign policy. American economic interests in Manchuria were small. Ironically, despite Japan's ability to undercut American goods, the fact that most residents of Manchuria's main port were Japanese, and that the United States gave moral and economic support to China, American trade with Manchuria tripled in the period 1932-40.

The Japanese considered their actions justified, especially because of the factors which combined to trigger their aggression. A key precipitant was the slump which followed the Wall Street Crash and the protectionist policies which were widely adopted around the world in response to it. Japan's exports fell by 43 per cent in value between 1929 and 1931. Deprived of American buyers for their silk, many Japanese farmers suffered great hardship. Japanese manufacturers laid off workers which increased social discontent. Such conditions boosted ultra-nationalist organisations and led to calls for a stronger foreign policy. Manchuria was the place where strength could be most readily demonstrated - Japan needed to regain control over her markets and resources in order to sustain her industry. At the same time, the Japanese army sought ways of implementing the policies it thought necessary for its defence by asserting its independence and resisting interference by the civil authorities. The Japanese military were concerned about Chinese attacks on Japan's privileges in Manchuria, in particular Jiang Jieshi's encouragement of Chinese people to move to Manchuria and his attempt to build a rival and parallel railway to compete with the Southern Manchurian Railway. The northwards expansion of Guomindang influence directly threatened the vast Japanese holdings in Manchuria and there were genuine fears that Chinese efforts to undermine the Japanese position in Manchuria might succeed. The loss of Manchuria was unthinkable from Japan's point of view. It would pose a threat to the Korean frontier and deprive Japan of Manchuria's resources of food and industrial raw materials.

For the United States the abstract question of American neutrality towards aggression became a real and pressing issue as the Chinese turned to them for support. Given the blatant violation of post-war principles and treaties, should the United States support the League of Nations in the name of collective security? What would such support entail? Should the United States remain aloof? What was the view of the American people? President Hoover, deeply concerned about the economic depression was clear that, facing catastrophe at home, the nation must avoid any risk of entanglement in a foreign war. Secretary of State Stimson at first hoped that the unilateral actions by the Japanese army would be checked by civilian leaders - 'My problem is to let the Japanese know that we are watching them and at the same time do it in a way which will help Shidehara who is on the right side, and not play in to the hands of nationalist agitators.' He overestimated the Japanese government's ability to rein in the military - by November 1931 he could write that 'the Japanese government which we have been dealing with is no longer in control' and that 'the situation is in the hands of mad dogs'. Whilst the League of Nations and the United States dallied the Japanese army continued to move through Manchuria.

America's main response to the crisis was the issuing of a non-recognition doctrine on 7 January 1932. Stimson declared that the United States would not recognise any agreement that China and Japan might enter that violated the principles of China's territorial or administrative integrity, the Open Door, and the Kellogg-Briand pact. Japan ignored this and on 28 January marched into Shanghai. Stimson went on to make public but empty threats to fortify Guam and build up the American navy in the Pacific if Japan did not halt its aggression. He resorted to lecture and bluff because he had few other options. Stimson's biographer concluded that he 'wound up like a man before a breaking dam with a shovel in his hands'. Stimson himself remarked that he was armed only with 'spears of straw and swords of ice'.

President Roosevelt endorsed the non-recognition of Japanese control by Henry Stimson, commenting in January 1933, 'American foreign policy must uphold the sanctity of international treaties. That is a cornerstone on which all relations between nations must rest.' Moral and political factors were paramount in adopting this approach. Every American town knew by 1933 that Japan had defied the League of Nations. The turning of Manchuria into the puppet state of Manchukuo in 1932 was followed by the well-publicised Japanese bombing of Shanghai. Had economic factors been the main consideration it is not certain that America would have sided with China. The United States had twice as much capital invested in Japan as in China in the early

1930s and enjoyed three times as much trade with Japan. Japan went on to defy the League of Nations Lytton Commission report which criticised the Japanese for their conduct in Manchuria and she withdrew from the League in early 1933.

How critical should we be of the American response to the Manchurian crisis? There is plenty to be said in their defence. The international community was in disarray at this time and the United States did not bear the obligations of a signatory of the League of Nations covenant. There was a legitimate concern that other countries were seeking, as Stimson put it, 'to leave the baby on America's doorstep'. Moreover, without high risk and considerable expenditure there was little that the United States, Britain, or France either singly or even collectively could have done to compel Japan to surrender its gains in Manchuria. At a purely practical level, Britain's economic stake in East Asia was too great and America's too small to risk challenging Japan's decided military superiority in the region. Public opinion supported President Hoover in his rejection of economic sanctions as entailing too great a risk of war, especially if the United States was venturing forth alone. Those Americans who wished for a more active policy to be pursued against Japan were a minority with little influence in Congress. However, having said this, speaking in retrospect in 1947 Stimson admitted that the doctrine of non-recognition and moral condemnation was wholly inadequate:

1 What happened after World War One was that we lacked the
  courage to enforce the authoritative decision of the international
  world. We agreed with the Kellogg Pact that aggressive war must
  end. We renounced it and we condemned those who might use it.
5 But it was a moral condemnation only. We thus did not reach the
  second half of the question - what will you do with an aggressor
  when you catch him? If we had reached it, we should easily have
  found the right answer, but that answer escaped us for it implied a
  duty to catch the criminal and such a choice meant war ... Our
10 offence was thus that of the man who passed by on the other side.

The American reaction to the Manchurian crisis was paralysed amidst the ruins of her economy and therefore the ruins of her entire post-war foreign policy in East Asia. The Roosevelt administration was to face many of the same constraints and problems in pursuing a non-military foreign policy.

5 Roosevelt and Japan, 1933-8

Drift, indecision, and passivity were the main features of America's East Asian policies in the 1930s. The United States was unprepared to agree to Japanese expansion (there was no recognition of Manchukuo) but no significant steps were taken to push it back. The British ambassador in Washington, after a conversation with the President, reported to London that FDR's 'view is that there is nothing to be done at present to stop [the] Japanese government and that the question can only be solved by the ultimate inability of Japan to stand the strain any longer. His policy would be to avoid anything that would tend to relieve that strain'. Little American action seemed required during the lull in fighting between China and Japan which lasted until July 1937. Roosevelt sought to hold foreign policy problems in Asia (and Europe) at bay as the depression forced him to concentrate on domestic relief and economic recovery. FDR has a well-deserved reputation as a great American President for the leadership he offered the country during the Great Depression and the Second World War but his approach to foreign policy could be maddeningly vague and inconsistent. One recent critic, Frederick Marks, sees Roosevelt as basing his foreign policy upon vague prejudices and shifting impulses - a diplomacy as insubstantial and fleeting as wind over sand. Policies were announced with an eye more to their domestic impact than to repercussions abroad. Arguably in East Asia his insensitivity to Japan's legitimate needs in Manchuria and China and his ambivalent but mainly pro-Chinese diplomacy pushed Japan into alliance with Germany and Italy and finally into war. On the other hand, the detailed recent assessment of Roosevelt's foreign policy by Robert Dallek concluded that 'too much has been made of Roosevelt's shortcomings and too little of the constraints under which he had to work in foreign affairs'. These constraints included American public outrage over Japanese conduct in China, which forced declarations of moral censure, and the strong degree of isolationism in Congress which limited his room for manoeuvre. What is clear is that moral condemnation had little impact on the Japanese. Ambassador Grew reported in February 1933 as the Japanese withdrew from the League of Nations:

1 The military themselves, and the public through military propaganda are fully prepared to fight rather than surrender to moral or other pressure from the West. The moral obloquy of the rest of the world serves only to strengthen not modify their 5 determination.

From the spring of 1933 to the summer of 1937 there was peace of a kind between China and Japan but there was no cessation of Japanese interference, economic and political, in the affairs of North China. By the summer of 1935 the five provinces of North China had submitted to Japanese rule, and in November they were formally detached from the Nationalist regime of Jiang Jieshi. At a Tokyo press conference in April 1934 a Japanese foreign office spokesman announced what appeared to be a Japanese 'Monroe Doctrine' warning foreign powers to keep their hands off China. The State Department responded very tolerantly and meekly to the statement. Secretary of State Cordell Hull asked the press to avoid stirring up trouble and directed his Far Eastern experts to suggest changes in America's China policy to reduce difficulties with Japan. Although Roosevelt's instincts were sympathetic to China and there was some financial aid (for example, $50 million credits agreed in May 1933), in the main America failed to assist China significantly until very late in the 1930s. Indeed, American financial policies at this time created further problems for China. As a device for easing the depression in the United States and of appeasing silver producing parts of the country such as Nevada, Congress enacted legislation raising the price the government would pay for silver. The Chinese currency was based upon silver and the new American policy threatened them with financial collapse with the potential flood of silver out of the country. The Chinese narrowly avoided fiscal disaster by a decree in November 1935 nationalising the metal and prohibiting its export but, despite this, the Chinese economy was significantly weakened, making it an easier prey for the Japanese.

In addition, American naval policies sent out mixed messages to Japan and naval strategy in the Pacific seemed to lack a sense of coherence. From the start of his Presidency Roosevelt was determined to keep Japan from increasing her naval strength relative to the United States. Under New Deal relief programmes in 1933 he allocated funds for 32 new vessels, including two aircraft carriers, and by 1937 naval appropriations had doubled. The United States was only building up to the limits of earlier treaties and Roosevelt was keen to keep the naval arms limitations intact. However, the American naval build-up convinced the Japanese in 1935 to end the treaty limitations, thus setting off a vigorous arms race. America was resolved not to accept either Japan's desire for equality or a major relaxation of the ratios in favour of Japan. At the same time, the Tydings-McDuffie Act of 1934 promised independence to the Philippines in 12 years, implying an American readiness to withdraw from the Western Pacific as a colonial power. Roosevelt also talked vaguely in November 1936 of disarming 'practically everything in the Pacific except Japan, Australia, New Zealand, and Singapore. This would leave the Philippines, Shanghai, Hong Kong, the Dutch East Indies, British North Borneo, and other important points neutralised'. While making judicious concessions to Japan, Roosevelt would have been well advised to shore up America's fortifications and naval presence in the Pacific.

An American trade commissioner in Shanghai in 1938 charged quite correctly that the 'Open Door' was being 'banged, barred, and bolted' and that Japanese expansion was being pursued without American retaliation. The United States share of Japanese exports fell from 37 per cent in 1925-9 to just over 14 per cent in 1935-9 but in 1938 America still supplied Japan with 44 per cent of its imports, a sizeable portion of which consisted of cars, machinery, copper, oil, iron, and steel. Japan sought control over markets and resources on the East Asian mainland in order to sustain her industry. The idea developed of building an autonomous Japanese bloc - which they described as a Greater East Asia Co-Prosperity Sphere. The different regions of North East Asia - Japan, Korea, Manchukuo, North China, and Taiwan - were to constitute a bloc within which heavy industry was to be developed. In 1938 Japan declared a 'New Order' for Asia which meant the ousting of Western imperialism and the creation of a self-sufficient Asian bloc united economically and racially. The rest of the area brought under Japanese rule - most of China, South-East Asia, and the islands of the south-west Pacific would serve as a source of raw materials and export earnings.

When full-scale hostilities broke out between Japan and China in July 1937, the initial American response was a vague declaration of principles from Cordell Hull. The United States' main concern was to avoid being caught in the crossfire of the China/Japan war. The State Department encouraged Americans to evacuate from the interior of China and discouraged ships from carrying aircraft and other arms to China. An American gunboat, the Panay, escorting three small oil tankers on the Yangtze river and standing by to evacuate embassy staff, was bombed and sunk by a Japanese aircraft on 12 December 1937. Far from stirring up a war spirit in the United States, the attack enabled one of the leading Pacifist Congressmen, Louis Ludlow of Indiana, to seek an amendment to the constitution stripping Congress of power to declare war 'until confirmed by a majority of all votes cast thereon in a nation-wide referendum'. The proposal was only narrowly voted down by 209:188. There was relief in Washington when the Japanese quickly apologised and offered reparations. Many Americans felt that the vessel should not have been there in the first place.

America refused to adopt a leadership role in foreign affairs in this period and effectively opted out. The British Prime Minister, Neville Chamberlain, noted in a private letter in December 1937 that 'it is always best and safest to count on the Americans for nothing but words'. The United States rejected no less than 10 British appeals between July and November 1937 to participate in a joint offer of mediation in the Sino-Japanese conflict or a show of naval strength. FDR remarked to a press conference in July 1937 that people were looking, 'for somebody outside of Europe to come forward with a hat and a rabbit in it ... Well ... I haven't got a hat and I haven't got a rabbit in it'. However, it seemed at one point as if Roosevelt had indeed produced such a 'rabbit'. Addressing a Chicago audience on 5 October 1937, he used a medical metaphor to describe American policy after the China incident. He called for a 'quarantine' on aggressors to check the 'epidemic of world lawlessness'. Americans, he declared, could not be safe in a 'world of disorder'. In fact, the President had no specific plan in mind for military or economic sanctions. The speech has been described by one historian as 'a confused and unsuccessful attempt to solve the dilemma of how to restrict aggression without resorting to threatening measures'. Defenders of Roosevelt argue that he showed a realistic appreciation that he lacked the means to satisfy the expectations aroused by his speech and that public sentiment remained a powerful bar to bringing meaningful pressure upon Japan. Public sentiment in 1937 ran 7:3 in favour of a withdrawal of American citizens from China in order to avoid the possibility of confrontation with Japan. In November 1937 Roosevelt sent American representatives to an international conference in Brussels but this turned into a futile debate about the need for a common attitude. The conference thundered against Japanese aggression at American instigation but, unwilling to align itself with Britain and France, the American government would go no further than verbalise its displeasure.

6 The Tortuous Road to War

The United States assumed a more active role in foreign affairs from 1938 onwards although it is difficult to pinpoint precisely when American policy moved from passivity into active opposition to Japan. One historian has described Roosevelt's policies aptly as a child's 'game of giant steps' in which the President moved 'two steps forward and one back before he took the giant step ahead'. Roosevelt was always concerned not to go too far ahead of public opinion. Policies that were directed against Japan rested upon the assumption that they would prevent rather than risk war. It was certainly the case that the significance of China in American thinking was revised upwards in 1938. US officials developed a primitive domino theory holding that the loss of China would 'undermine the entire Western position right across Southeast Asia and the Pacific'. Using Presidential discretion, Roosevelt chose not to apply the neutrality acts (see page 75) to the war in China. The application of the law would have principally affected China which needed American arms and loans. An oil loan of $25 million to China in December 1938 has been seen as a turning point in American East Asian policy. This was the first concrete measure which the US government took in an attempt to restrain post-1937 Japanese expansion. This followed the bold announcement in Tokyo of a Japanese intention to create a 'new order in East Asia'. The policy clearly contradicted 'Open Door' principles and was a euphemism for Japanese control of China. The United States was to provide China with millions of dollars of additional aid as the Japanese advanced in 1940-41. The largest package of assistance was announced after the temporary closure of the Burma Road supply route to China in October 1940. America subsequently agreed a loan of $250 million and agreed to provide 1,000 planes on credit.

There has been much debate amongst historians as to whether there was any way out of the escalating antagonism between the United States and Japan in the diplomacy of the last three or four years before the outbreak of the Pacific War. Many historians argue that the United States missed opportunities to heal the breach between the two countries or at least to calm relations. At the time there were widening differences between those in charge of East Asian affairs at the State Department and Joseph Grew's embassy staff in Tokyo about the best way to deal with Japan. Ambassador Grew consistently called for a conciliatory policy. He opposed economic sanctions against Japan on the grounds that by pushing Japan into a corner they would make war more likely. He supported the various peace overtures which were made in 1940-41. In a strongly worded telegram to Washington in December 1939 he wrote:

1 The simple fact is that we are here dealing not with a unified Japan but with a Japanese Government which is endeavouring courageously, even with only gradual success, to fight against a recalcitrant Japanese army, a battle which happens to be our battle
5 ... If we now rebuff the Government we shall not be serving to discredit the Japanese army but rather to furnish the army with powerful arguments to be used in its own support. I am convinced that we are in a position either to direct American-Japanese relations into a progressively healthy channel or to accelerate their
10 movement straight down hill.

Hard-liners led by Stanley Hornbeck of the State Department hoped and expected that by hardening economic sanctions with oil and trade embargoes the United States could force Japan into submission. In a memorandum issued the day after Grew's telegram Hornbeck argued:

1 In my opinion adoption as a major premise of thought that the 'civilian' element in the Japanese nation, may gain an ascendancy over the 'military' element and, having done so, would alter the objectives of Japanese policy can lead to nothing but error and
5 confusion in reasoning ... Practically the whole of the Japanese population believes in and is enthusiastic over the policy of expansion and aggrandisement of the Japanese empire.

He urged policy makers to believe that the Japanese were insincere. Grew had been on the Japanese scene for almost a decade whereas Hornbeck did not know Japan and was strongly pro-Chinese. Nevertheless, Secretary of State Hull and official American policy became increasingly sympathetic to Hornbeck's view.

America progressively turned the economic screws on Japan. There was a firm belief in the United States that increasingly tough trade sanctions would eventually force the Japanese to withdraw from China

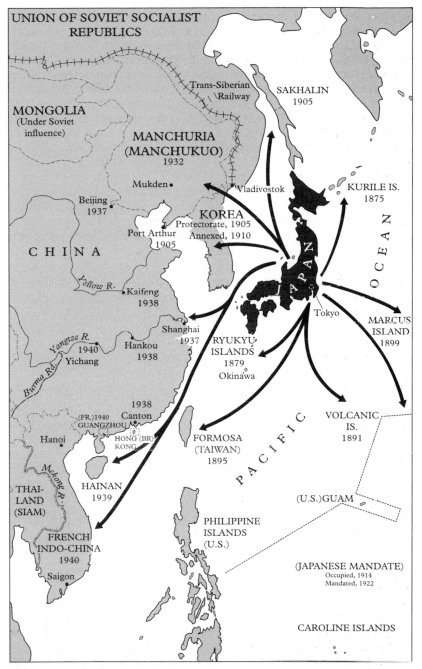

UNION OF SOVIET SOCIALIST
REPUBLICS

MONGOLIA
(Under Soviet
influence)

Trans-Siberian
Railway

SAKHALIN
1905

MANCHURIA
(MANCHUKUO)
1932

Mukden

Vladivostok

KURILE IS.
1875

Beijing
1937

KOREA
Protectorate, 1905
Annexed, 1910

Port Arthur
1905

C H I N A

Yellow R.

Kaifeng
1938

Shanghai
1937

JAPAN

Tokyo

MARCUS
ISLAND
1899

Yangtze R.

1940
Yichang

Hankou
1938

RYUKYU
ISLANDS
1879
Okinawa

Burma Rd.

1938

Canton

(FR.)1940
GUANGZHOU

Hanoi

HONG (BR)
KONG

FORMOSA
(TAIWAN)
1895

VOLCANIC
IS.
1891

PACIFIC

O C E A N

Mekong R.

THAI-
LAND
(SIAM)

HAINAN
1939

(U.S.)GUAM

FRENCH
INDO-CHINA
1940

Saigon

PHILIPPINE
ISLANDS
(U.S.)

(JAPANESE MANDATE)
Occupied, 1914
Mandated, 1922

CAROLINE ISLANDS

Japanese expansion until 1941

and cause them to abandon their aims in Asia. There were also
international and domestic pressures to introduce stronger economic
measures. An opinion poll in June 1938 showed 84 per cent against the
continued export of military goods. In the spring of 1939 Congress
pressured Roosevelt by the introduction of a resolution authorising
restrictions on trade with nations violating the Nine Power Agreement
of 1922. A majority of the Senate Foreign Relations Committee by 1940
campaigned for an embargo on all trade. Nevertheless, for a long time
American policy-makers were cautious about going as far as this. They
feared weakening Japanese moderates and for a long time did not
impose oil sanctions for fear of forcing Japan into a military expedition
against the Dutch East Indies. Economic sanctions, however, did
contribute to worsening US-Japanese relations. In rapid succession the
American government announced in January 1939 a 'moral embargo'
on planes and aviation parts sales and in February 1939 a cessation of
credit. In July 1939 a long-standing trade agreement with Japan was
suspended. In July 1940 a partial trade embargo was announced on
aviation and motor fuel, lubricants, and high grade melting scrap.
Finally, in July 1941 there was a further beefing up of sanctions as the
Japanese entered IndoChina. A freezing order was placed upon all
Japanese assets in the United States. There was some ambiguity as to
whether this was intended to close off all oil exports but a total embargo
emerged haphazardly. American policies in this period had the effect of
creating a siege mentality within the Japanese leadership that led to the
argument that the only solution to the American, British, and Dutch oil
blockade was war.

   Of course, American policies towards Japan prior to Pearl Harbor
need to be understood within an international as much as an East Asian
context. There was an interconnection between developments in
Europe and Asia. The German victories in the spring and summer of
1940 engendered in even moderate Japanese leaders what Foreign
Minister Togo described as a fear of 'missing the bus'. As Grew noted in
his journal in August 1940, 'The German military machine and system
and their brilliant successes have gone to the Japanese head like strong
wine.' The collapse of France touched off a new round of Japanese
aggression. Japan declared the regions of the South Seas part of her
Greater Co-Prosperity Sphere. The sense of danger for the United
States increased in September 1940 when Japan entered into a tripartite
alliance with the European fascist powers Germany and Italy and started
making moves into French Indo-China. Once Japan joined the Axis
alliance the United States could no longer isolate German from Japanese
aggression. Certain that American strategic priorities lay across the
Atlantic in Europe (the Lend-Lease Act was agreed in March 1941) the
Roosevelt administration hoped to avoid a two-front war. FDR was
eager to extend diplomatic negotiations with Tokyo in 1941 as a means
of putting off war in the Pacific as long as possible. His continuing

concern was that scarce resources be marshalled to fight Hitler. Control of the Atlantic was in doubt in 1941 - Roosevelt noted 'I simply have not got enough Navy to go round - and every little episode in the Pacific means fewer ships in the Atlantic.' Another explanation of why Roosevelt and Hull were stalling on Japanese peace overtures whilst tightening the oil embargo from mid-1941 was so that Japan would not dare to attack the Soviet Union from the Siberian side, thus allowing Moscow to use its Siberian forces to help hold off Hitler in Europe. American policies thus need to be seen in an international context.

It is debatable to what extent American policies had the capacity to alter Japanese intentions in the years leading up to Pearl Harbor. Some historians take the view that Hornbeck was right in his hard-line assessment of Japan and that all Japanese political leaders, including civilians, agreed with the military's aims. The issuing of the 'New Order', the agreement with the Axis powers, and the move into Indo-China seemed to confirm this analysis. A more widespread view is that Japanese ministers would have preferred to avoid war with the United States and Britain but were prepared to face war if it became in their judgcment unavoidable. There was a genuine debate within successive Japanese administrations over whether to join Germany by invading Soviet Siberia or to gain their principal objectives in China and South-East Asia through negotiations with the United States. Japanese navy leaders knew that in their simulated war games with the United States Japan invariably lost. It has been argued that Japanese leaders' reluctance to undertake southern expansion is revealed in their failure to map out a strategy for occupying and administering Indo-China, Malaya, and the Dutch East Indies. The Hull-Nomura peace talks between February and June 1941 held out some possibility of a settlement. Admiral Nomura accepted his appointment as ambassador to the United States in January 1941 only after he had been assured by Premier Konoe that the highest naval authorities sincerely sought improved relations with the United States. Emperor Hirohito had a genuine reluctance to resort to war and was keen to explore every diplomatic avenue. Even after the Japanese invasion of Indo-China, the American imposition of a full trade embargo, and the breaking off of the Nomura talks, the Japanese government made last-ditch efforts to avoid war. From early August 1941 formula after formula was proposed. A peace conference between Premier Konoe and Roosevelt in the Pacific was proposed. Unofficial diplomacy was engaged in through back-channels, although Secretary of State Hull took a haughty attitude of disdain towards the efforts of two American Catholic priests Father James Drought and Bishop James Walsh in their work with pcacc-sccking groups in Tokyo. Given the distance between the basic principles and outlook of Japanese and American leaders at this time the prospects of a negotiated agreement were thin. The ghost of Munich haunted the West. It appeared only too likely that an American-Japanese settlement would be unattainable save at the expense of China. Thus the various peace projects came to nothing. Nevertheless, it seemed to be a basic premise within the State Department that the Japanese would not risk war with the United States and that therefore no compromise was necessary. This was a misjudgement. American diplomatic actions unwittingly discouraged the Japanese from accommodation and played into the hands of Japanese ultra-nationalists.

Relations between America and Japan deteriorated considerably in the second half of 1941. The key turning point was the decision reached at a high level Japanese conference on 2 July that Japan should proceed with the invasion of Indo-China even if it meant going to war with Britain and the United States. At the beginning of September another conference of Japanese military and civilian leaders formally agreed that the country must be prepared for war unless, through peace talks in Washington, the economic blockade was eased by the middle of October. It was a decision reached in a mood of desperation. Either diplomacy would have to eliminate the barriers to trade erected by the Americans, or the Japanese would have to seize sources of material and act before the economic sanctions and weather conditions hindered their ability to fight. In October, War Minister Tojo replaced Konoe as Japanese Premier and from this point peace negotiations, though not devoid of good faith, had to be viewed against a cascade of war preparations. Roosevelt was aware of Japanese plans because their diplomatic cables could be read by a code-breaking device called 'Magic' (the intercepted messages encouraged the Americans to see the Japanese peace suggestions as insincere). America and Japan's final proposals underlined the gulf between them. The Japanese hoped for a standstill agreement with Washington; in return for their withdrawal from South Indo-China the United States would restore normal commercial relations. The American Chiefs of Staff favoured acceptance of the proposal which at least had the merit of buying America time. Roosevelt and Hull decided to maintain a firm front. The reply to Tokyo of 26 November 1941, which became known as the 'Hull Note' emphasised that America required a withdrawal not just from Indo-China but from China itself. It was diplomatic deadlock and it appeared that nothing now could put the engines of war into reverse.

7 Pearl Harbor

The Japanese launched their attack on Pearl Harbor because they thought that they had no alternative but to fight, although they were far from certain they could win. An Imperial statement on the declaration of war issued on 8 December summarised Japanese motives:

1 Eager for a realisation of their inordinate ambition to dominate the

orient, both America and Britain, giving support to the [Chinese] regime, have aggravated disturbances in East Asia. Moreover, these two powers, inducing other countries to follow suit,
5 increased military preparations on all sides of our Empire to challenge us. They have obstructed by every means our peaceful commerce, and finally resorted to a direct severance of economic relations, menacing gravely the existence of our Empire. Patiently
10 have we waited and long have we endured in the hope that our government might retrieve the situation in peace, but our adversaries, showing not the least spirit of conciliation, have unduly delayed a settlement.

Pushed into a corner, the Japanese preferred the strategy of surprise attack to the alternative of humiliating diplomatic concession.

In the years after Pearl Harbor, critics of Roosevelt's leadership argued that the President had provoked the Japanese attack as a 'backdoor' to the European war. There is little doubt that by the middle of 1941 Roosevelt had been convinced by Winston Churchill of the dangers of Nazi control over continental Europe. Some critics even suggested that FDR expected the Pearl Harbor raid but allowed American forces to be surprised in order to ensure unity at home. This latter idea can be dismissed. It rests upon a poorly substantiated claim that American radio operators tracked mysterious signals from the Pearl Harbor task force but that these were suppressed by US intelligence. It is highly unlikely that Japanese radio silence was compromised. Even if one accepts the notion that a plot did exist to lure the Japanese into striking first, it was not necessary to leave every US battleship of the Pacific Fleet in port, defenceless at anchor. Plans for the Pearl Harbor raid had been discussed in Japanese naval circles as early as January 1941 and later there had been secret exercises at Kagoshima where the bay reproduced to some extent the features of the American Hawaiian base. There is no need to doubt Roosevelt's genuine shock when news of the attack reached him - he described the event as 'a date which will live in infamy'. Among the Americans in December 1941 there was much evidence of incompetence, mistakes, and miscalculations but not of provable conspiracy.

Why did the United States, which in the 1930s watched in passive disapproval while Japan's massive war effort against China proceeded, react so firmly to the Japanese occupation of French Indo-China which, almost alone of the advances of the previous decade, took place with the agreement of the country concerned and largely without bloodshed? Two explanations have about equal weight. With the move into Indo-China, Japan now clearly threatened Southeast Asia; it was against America's strategic interest that Japan should dominate the Western Pacific, while being able to call upon huge supplies of strategic raw materials. The second reason was related to the European war. The

Japanese move into Indo-China threatened to cut off British access to resources to the south and west just when they were essential to the struggle against Germany. Roosevelt knew that the imposition of sanctions rendered war virtually inevitable. Four days after Pearl Harbor, Germany and Italy, under Japanese prompting, declared war on America as a gesture of allied solidarity. The Japanese attack on Pearl Harbor, coupled with Hitler's ritual but very unwise declaration of war on America, made it possible for the United States to enter the European war promptly. That this was uppermost in Roosevelt's mind is supported by the way most American forces were swiftly assigned to the European theatre not the Far East.

However successful in immediate military terms the Pearl Harbor attack proved to be, it was one of history's greatest military blunders. There were many consequences of the 'Day of Infamy' but there was no possibility of a successful Japanese invasion of the American west coast. American air power at home was capable of dealing with any attempted invasion. The attack served to unite the American people for a war against Japan as nothing else could have. Congress agreed to Roosevelt's request for a Declaration of War on 8 December with only one dissenting vote.

Making Notes on *'The USA and Japan : The Road to Pearl Harbor'*

Your notes for this chapter might be organized around six key questions:
1   What were American interests in East Asia in the 1920s and 1930s?
2   Why were relations between America and Japan generally quite good in the 1920s?
3   Why did Japan pursue expansionist policies in the 1930s?
4   What evidence is there to support the statement in the text that 'drift, indecision, and passivity were the main features of America's East Asian policies in the 1930s'?
5   What actions might American policy-makers have taken in the 1930s and early years of the Second World War to avoid what eventually occurred in December 1941?
6   Why did Japan gamble on an all-out attack on the American fleet at Pearl Harbor?

In the light of past experience, examiners are most likely to be concerned with the latter three questions but the first three questions represent important contextual background. The chapter sub-headings should direct you to the relevant sections of the text. When addressing the question of American interests in East Asia you need to consider strategic, economic, and humanitarian/ideological concerns. You should also ask yourself why America felt it necessary to concern itself with events in China in this period. The Washington Treaties were clearly a central plank of US-Japanese relations in the 1920s - you need

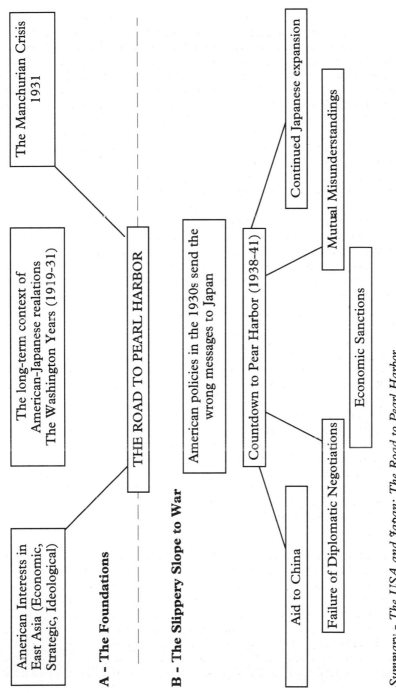

The Manchurian Crisis
1931

The long-term context of
American-Japanese realations
The Washington Years (1919-31)

THE ROAD TO PEARL HARBOR

A - The Foundations

American Interests in
East Asia (Economic,
Strategic, Ideological)

B - The Slippery Slope to War

American policies in the 1930s send the
wrong messages to Japan

Continued Japanese expansion

Mutual Misunderstandings

Countdown to Pear Harbor (1938-41)

Economic Sanctions

Aid to China

Failure of Diplomatic Negotiations

Summary - The USA and Japan: The Road to Pearl Harbor

to understand the key elements of the various agreements. After making a list of the reasons for Japanese expansion in the 1930s, you might consider the view that Western policies pushed Japan in a militaristic direction.

As a preliminary exercise to making notes on the last three questions you might find it helpful to engage with the events and issues confronting American policy-makers in a more active way. Recent research has suggested that people remember about 10 per cent of what they see (or write down), 40 per cent of what they discuss, and about 90 per cent of what they do. A problem-solving, role-play exercise, focusing upon the options open to the United States in responding to Japanese aggression, should help you to gain an appreciation of the difficulties faced by American leaders. Working in groups of four or five you need to see yourself as American government advisers each of whom is advocating different responses to Japanese actions. Your group meets on four different occasions: in 1931 following the Japanese attack on Manchuria, in 1937 after the Japanese declaration of war on China, in September 1940 after Japan entered the Axis alliance, and in July 1941 after Japan entered Indo-China. There are a range of possible courses of action. The United States might for example, ignore Japanese actions, take diplomatic action, lobby for an international diplomatic response, apply economic sanctions, toughen economic sanctions, prepare for military action, or take military action. The government might eventually adopt a combination of these responses. Individuals in your group should each prepare a advisory memorandum based on a different course of action and present it to the rest of the group. Be prepared to defend your point of view!

United States policy towards Japan developed in a series of small steps. You need to have a clear appreciation of the ways in which international relations was rapidly changing between 1937 and 1941 during the immediate approach of war and the early years of conflict in East Asia and Europe. Look back at your notes on chapter 4 and identify the key international events which took place in the four years before Pearl Harbor. Briefly state how each one affected US policy towards Japan.

Answering essay questions on *'The USA and Isolation 1921-41'* and *'The USA and Japan'*

There are a number of themes discussed in this chapter which are popular topics with examiners. For most possible questions you will need to have an understanding of American attitudes and actions in both East Asia and Europe so you should not attempt to plan answers to the essay questions listed below until you have read and taken notes on Chapters 4 and 5. You might be asked to analyse the nature or extent of American isolationism in this period. For example:

1 Account for the strength of isolationist sentiment in America in the period from 1920 to 1939.
2 'The idea that America was isolated from international affairs in the inter-war years is a myth'. Discuss.

Alternatively, the policies, personality, and decisions of Franklin Delano Roosevelt might provide the main focus of attention. For example:

3 'A naive and unskilled practitioner in foreign affairs'. Is this an accurate assessment of FDR between 1933 and 1941?

Sometimes quotations like this can be intimidating but don't be put off. Use the quotations as a direct guide to your response. Draw up a list of factors to support the quotation and a list of factors to counter it. Alongside the points for each side briefly note relevant details and examples which you would include in your answer. Remember to reach an overall judgement and that there is no 'right' or 'expected' answer.

The reasons why America went to war in December 1941 provides another popular topic. For example:

4 To what degree was American intervention in the Second World War inspired by democratic idealism?
5 Why did the USA enter the Second World War against both Japan and Germany?

More complex questions will link isolationism, Roosevelt, and/or the American entry into the Second World War in different ways. For example:

6 To what extent should FDR be blamed for America's isolationist policies in the 1930s?
7 Why was isolationist sentiment unable to prevent the entry of the United States into the Second World War?
8 To what extent was FDR intent on taking the USA into the war before 7 December 1941?

The essay-writing advice in this section is mainly intended to help you to improve the quality of the 'meat' of your essay which is sandwiched between the introduction and conclusion. Having identified five or six key themes, you need to pay close attention to the order in which your paragraphs appear in the plan. Your aim is to devise a structure to enable paragraphs 'naturally' to succeed one another, with logical connections. If the first sentence of each paragraph is an analytical rather than a factual statement this will ensure that you are directly addressing the question throughout the essay. For example, one approach to Question 7 might look like this:

Paragraph 1: Isolationist tendencies in America, shared by policy-makers and public opinion, had prevented America from responding to Japanese and German aggression throughout the 1930s ...

Paragraph 2: Isolationist sentiment, founded upon a range of deep-felt emotions and attitudes, continued to be powerful even after the outbreak of war in Europe in September 1939 ...

Paragraph 3: One of the main reasons that the America First organisation, the leading isolationist pressure group, began to lose ground was because President Roosevelt became increasingly convinced of the necessity of a close relationship with the powers who were fighting against German and Japanese militarism. His leadership and policies after 1939 edged the United States closer to war ...

Paragraph 4: Opinion in America could hardly ignore the expansion of the Axis powers and the future threat that this might pose the American interests. Isolationist sentiment diminished somewhat in the light of international events in 1940 and 1941 ...

Paragraph 5: America was close to war with Germany and Japan throughout 1941 but isolationist sentiment meant that Roosevelt still had to proceed cautiously. After Pearl Harbor even fervent supporters of American isolationism supported American entry into the Second World War ...

Try to produce a similar paragraph plan for Question 8. Next, flesh each paragraph out with at least four telling facts or details which support the generalisations in the opening sentences of the paragraph. Although sustained analysis is the prime requirement of examination essays, answers can appear superficial if they are not underpinned by an appropriate depth and range of knowledge.

Source-based questions *'The USA and Japan: The Road to Pearl Harbor'*

1 The American reaction to the Manchurian Crisis
Study the comments on the Manchurian Crisis by President Hoover (page 105) and Secretary of State Stimson (page 111).
a) What were America's 'obligations to China'? (5 marks)
b) What did Hoover mean in 1932 when he said 'civilisation is already weak enough'? (4 marks)
c) Explain Stimson's comment in 1932 that he was armed only with 'spears of straw and swords of ice'? (4 marks)
d) How far do you agree with the opinion voiced in 1947 by Stimson that America's response to the Manchurian Crisis was 'that of the man who passed by on the other side'? (7 marks)

2 Disagreements amongst American Foreign Policy advisers over American-Japanese relations in 1939
Read the views of Joseph Grew (Ambassador to Japan) and Stanley Hornbeck (State Department expert on East Asia) (page 116)
a) What reasons are given by Grew to support his argument that a conciliatory policy should be followed towards Japan? (5 marks)
b) Compare Grew's telegram with the memorandum issued by Hornbeck. In what ways and why did Hornbeck disagree with Grew's analysis? (6 marks)
c) An issue of contention which lay behind the Grew/Hornbeck difference of opinion was the merits of economic sanctions. List the arguments for and against imposing economic sanctions upon Japan. Which adviser do you feel has the better of the argument? (9 marks)

3 Japanese motives for declaring war on America
Read the Imperial Statement on the declaration of war issued on 8 December 1941 (pages 120-1)
a) What evidence is there to support the Japanese view that America had an 'inordinate ambition to dominate the orient'? (5 marks)
b) How far do you agree that the Americans showed 'not the least spirit of conciliation' in their dealings with Japan in 1940-41? (7 marks)
c) Was 'a settlement' of the issues which divided America and Japan possible or had war become inevitable by September 1940? (8 marks)

CHAPTER 6

The USA and the Second World War

1 Introduction

Winston Churchill, the British Prime Minister, rejoiced at the news of
the entry of the United States into the Second World War: 'Hitler's fate
was sealed. Mussolini's fate was sealed. As for the Japanese, they would
be ground to powder. All the rest was merely the application of
overwhelming force.' Ultimately his confidence was justified. The sheer
weight of resources and economic power which the Americans brought
to the Allied war effort totally altered the overall balance of forces.
Nevertheless, it was to take some time for America's 'overwhelming
force' to make itself felt and the immediate outlook in December 1941
was bleak.

The United States was unprepared for war. The navy was temporarily
crippled at Pearl Harbor and the army draft had been in place for only
just over a year. The expanding corps of civilians were ill-equipped and
lacked training. American industry was only partially converted from
peacetime production and many of the armaments that had been
produced had been sent overseas as Lend-Lease. For six months after
Pearl Harbor Japanese forces ran rampant in the Pacific and South East
Asia. They overwhelmed the European colonial empires and threatened
China, India, Australia, and Hawaii. The rapid fall of Singapore in
February 1942, which had been thought impregnable, was a particular
shock to the British. Churchill described it as 'the worst disaster and
largest capitulation of British history'. Nazi Germany controlled
continental Western Europe and looked set to take Soviet Russia as their
army battled towards the Caucasus. Elsewhere German forces under
Rommel seemed close to driving British army units out of Egypt whilst
in the Atlantic U-Boats sank more ships than the Allies could build. The
territorial gains of the Axis powers meant that winning the war - even
with the United States throwing its weight into the equation - would be
no easy or quick task.

After American entry into the Second World War, Great Britain, the
United States, and the Soviet Union formed the power-base of a
fifty-nation Grand Alliance. The signatories to the 'Declaration of the
United Nations' in January 1942 promised to fight together until the
Axis powers were defeated. Through extensive correspondence and
summit meetings (notably at Teheran in January 1943 and Yalta in
February 1945), the allied leaders Churchill, Franklin D. Roosevelt, and
Joseph Stalin not only plotted military strategy to defeat Germany, Italy,
and Japan but also shaped plans for the post-war era. Although the Allies
co-operated sufficiently to win the war, there were often sharp

differences expressed over war strategy, likely future territorial changes, and the post-war structure of international relations. There were disagreements, for example, on the opening of a second military front in Western Europe (delay increased Stalin's suspicions that America and Britain were content to let Russia bear the brunt of German aggression), the location of new military campaigns, and the quantity and availability of US supplies under the Lend-Lease programme. Moreover, there was jockeying for political position in the countries freed from Nazi and Japanese control, such as Poland and China. There was also debate on colonial issues; Roosevelt spoke frequently about ending European empires and granting independence to colonial peoples. He was thinking particularly about the role of France in Indo-China but also of Britain in India. Soon after defeating the Axis, the Grand Alliance broke apart and in the process generated the sources of a new conflict - the Cold War. The world in 1945 and the American place in that world was to be very different from the world of the inter-war years. America's military power, economic resources, and cultural influence were more pronounced than ever before.

It is worth underlining and exemplifying the extent of American economic power because ultimately it was the ability of the United States to mobilise its natural resources and huge reserves of manpower which was the key factor in the success of the allied war effort. By the end of the war 15 million men and several hundred thousand women had left their civilian lives for service in the military. Americans, virtually unaided, had beaten Japan back across the Pacific while providing leadership and more than half the men for the attack on Hitler. By D-Day in June 1944 the United States had more than 1.5 million soldiers stationed in England, and three of the six divisions assigned to make the initial Normandy landings were American. Aside from its fighting forces, however, America's greatest contribution to the allied war effort was its ability to produce vast quantities of everything that was required. The American economy had emerged from the gloom of the Great Depression before Pearl Harbor but full mobilisation produced spectacular results. The United States was truly the 'arsenal of victory', providing billions of dollars worth of arms for Britain, Russia, China, and dozens of smaller countries. Mass production techniques were developed for fighter aircraft, aircraft carriers, merchant vessels, trucks, and jeeps. This had a direct bearing on the course of the war. In the critical years of the Battle of the Atlantic the Allies lost 8.3 million tons of shipping in 1942 and 4 million tons in 1943, but these totals were compensated by Allied launchings of 7 million and 8 million tons respectively. United States shipbuilding capacity meant that merchant vessels could be replaced more quickly than U-Boats could sink them. The most telling statistics relate to aircraft production - without command of the air it was impossible for armies and navies to operate effectively. By 1943-4 the United States could produce an aircraft every five minutes. On D-Day itself the Germans could muster only 319 aircraft against the Allies 12,837.

Moreover, the contribution was qualitative as well as quantitative. American technological advances resulted in faster and more powerful fighter planes and more manoeuvrable aircraft carriers and battleships. The introduction of the proximity fuse early in 1943 - a radio device that caused shells to explode if they passed even close to the target - provided surface vessels with protection against air attack. The United States alone had the productive and technical capacity not only to wage two large scale conventional wars but also to invest the scientists, raw materials, and money (about $2 billion) in development of the atomic bomb, a new weapon which might or might not have worked. The efficient harnessing and expansion of America's productive capacity, stimulated and co-ordinated through a series of labour-management boards like the Office of Production Management and the War Labour Board was a major factor in the Allied Victory.

What, apart from defeating the enemy, was the war all about from the United States' point of view? What could the American people look forward to achieving by sending their young men to fight and die in far away places? President Roosevelt was careful not to articulate specific visions of the postwar world; he did not want to make hasty commitments or raise false hopes and wished to focus all of the nation's energy and attention on the task of winning the war. Having said this, broad goals were set out. The President provided a brief definition of American aims even before the United States entered the conflict. In a speech before Congress in January 1941 he called for a world based upon the 'four essential freedoms'; freedom of speech, freedom of religion, and freedom from want and fear. In August 1941 he and Churchill proclaimed the Atlantic Charter, a list of goals resembling Woodrow Wilson's Fourteen Points, including self-determination, Free Trade, and freedom of the seas. Sumner Welles, a State Department official, echoed a main theme in American public opinion when he declared in May 1942, 'Our victory must bring in its train the liberation of all peoples.' Cordell Hull, the Secretary of State until 1944, told a joint session of Congress in November 1943, following a mission to see Stalin in Moscow, that: 'There will no longer be any need for spheres of influence, for alliances, for balance of power, or any of the other special arrangements through which in the unhappy past, the nations strove to safeguard their security or to promote their interests.' Roosevelt was less idealistic than this - he looked to great power post-war control through what he called privately the 'four policemen' (the United States, the Soviet Union, Britain and China). His objectives included an expanded role for the United States in world affairs, particularly in Asia and the Pacific, Soviet-American co-operation to help preserve the peace, China's emergence as a strong force for peace in Asia, the gradual demise of colonial empires, leading eventually to independent states in

Asia and Africa, and an expansion of markets for American exports.

Historical debate about American diplomacy and actions between Pearl Harbor and the dropping of the atomic bombs on Hiroshima and Nagasaki in August 1945, which prompted the Japanese surrender and effectively ended the Second World War, has focused on a number of key areas. Perceptions of the performance of Roosevelt stand at the centre of any discussion of United States policy and the record of the Grand Alliance between 1941 and 1945. The focus upon presidential actions is justifiable - the State Department and Congress were sidelined when it came to making the key strategic decisions. Roosevelt did not make it easy for historians struggling to work out his underlying convictions and principles, depicting himself thus to a special study group in May 1942: 'You know I am a juggler, and I never let my right hand know what my left hand does ... I have one policy for Europe and one diametrically opposite for North and South America. I may be entirely inconsistent, and furthermore I am perfectly willing to mislead and tell untruths if it will help to win the war.'

Some scholars treat his record favourably, emphasising his grasp of power realities, his understanding of both the limits and opportunities of power, his deft handling of Churchill and Stalin to keep the alliance together, and his skill in finding a way through the unique complexities of conducting a global war. Other well qualified observers take a much more critical view of Roosevelt's diplomacy, particularly his handling of the relationship with the Soviet Union. George Kennan, for example, damned Roosevelt's foreign policy as that of 'a very superficial man, ignorant, dilettantish, severely limited in intellectual horizon'. The early part of this chapter will present the prosecution and defence cases on Roosevelt's conduct of the war effort. Subsequent sections will consider other central questions. How did America win the Pacific war against Japan? How justifiable was the decision of Roosevelt's successor, President Truman, to drop the atomic bomb? Why did the wartime alliance with the Soviet Union break down so rapidly, inaugurating a Cold War that would endure for over four decades? (Roosevelt has been condemned by many critics since the Second World War for refusing to treat the Soviet Union as an enemy during the latter stages of the war). How did American leaders view the position of their country in the world in 1945 and how in turn was America perceived by others?

2 FDR's Wartime Leadership: The Case for the Prosecution

Most aspects of American wartime diplomacy have been criticised at one time or another. Some of the criticisms emerge from more general assessments of Roosevelt's diplomatic style and personality. He has been depicted, for example, as essentially a political lightweight dominated early in the war by Churchill and later tricked by the wily Soviet leader. Certainly the British Prime Minister succeeded in postponing the main Allied attack in Western Europe until Anglo-American strength was overwhelming. US army chiefs and the Defence Secretary, Henry Stimson, regarded British strategy as peripheral to the main task of confronting Germany directly in Western Europe and as being calculated to serve British imperial interests. Some, such as General George Marshall, questioned the 'Atlantic First' strategy agreed with Churchill. Nearly every American military planner believed that the campaign in North Africa in 1942 provided inadequate relief for Russia and was an unnecessary diversion from the main purpose of striking at Hitler. One leading general complained, 'The Limeys have his ear, while we have the hind tit.' Whenever Roosevelt tentatively raised the question of the future status of India Churchill reacted angrily and discouraged further discussion of the issue. Moreover, the tensions of the Cold War years after 1945 led millions of Americans to criticise the policy of alliance with the USSR and FDR's tactics of accommodation as too soft. William Bullitt, America's first ambassador to the Soviet Union, wrote an article in Life magazine in August 1948 entitled 'How we Won the War and Lost the Peace'. According to this view, Roosevelt failed to understand the ruthless and aggressive nature of the Soviet regime, ignored the ideological implications of Marxist-Leninism, and made too many unnecessary concessions at the Yalta Conference. He gave Stalin the impression that the United States would probably withdraw into partial isolation after victory had been achieved, leading to the conclusion that the Soviet Union need not worry about American opposition to her post-war ambitions in Eastern Europe.

A further criticism which might be levelled at Roosevelt is that of a certain superficiality in his approach and a tendency to duck critical issues. This criticism might be supported by a detailed focus on his policies towards China and Poland. He instinctively shied away from problems that needed to be confronted, hoping for a solution to turn up. Moreover, even when he did explore solutions, he thought that conflicts of national interest could be overcome by discreet one-to-one bargaining and placed too much confidence in his personal charm winning over Stalin. One biographer, James MacGregor Burns, argued that there was a mismatch between Roosevelt's lofty words and his limited means. This, he argued, widened the gap between popular expectations and actual possibilities. Not only did this derangement of ends and means lead to crushed hopes, disillusion, and cynicism at home, but it helped sow the seeds of the Cold War during World War Two, as the Kremlin contrasted Roosevelt's coalition rhetoric with his Atlantic First strategy and falsely suspected a bourgeois conspiracy to destroy Soviet Communism; and Indians and Chinese contrasted Roosevelt's anticolonial words with his military concessions to colonial powers, and falsely inferred that he was an imperialist at heart and a hypocrite to boot.

On the latter topic, Harold Macmillan, Churchill's chief diplomatic adviser in North Africa at the Casablanca conference of January 1943 reported that, 'The President talked a great deal about colonial aspirations towards independence and the approaching end of 'imperialism'. All this was equally embarrassing to the British and to the French'. In September 1941 Churchill had announced to the British parliament that the Atlantic Charter applied to the enemy but not to India and Burma. In November 1942 he made a much-publicised comment that he had not become Prime Minister 'in order to preside over the liquidation of the British empire'. Some conclude that Roosevelt said much about decolonisation but did little. By the end of the war Roosevelt seemed to have backed away from his determination to liberate colonial peoples. A trusteeship plan presented at the Yalta conference provided for placing under the United Nations only those territories taken from the defeated Axis powers, or those voluntarily put under international control by the colonial powers.

There is a case for saying that Roosevelt was so preoccupied with the military problems of the war that he gave insufficient thought to the diplomatic and political problems involved. The American President's policy on the future of Poland, for example, appears weak all the way down the line, both in respect to its territorial boundaries and on the question of the government of the country after the war. Roosevelt viewed the London-based Polish government-in-exile as unhelpful troublemakers. He never appointed an ambassador to the London Poles. He conceded at the Tehran Conference that Polish affairs were 'of special concern' to Stalin. Prime Minister Sikorski warned shortly after this that if Stalin's pretensions went unchallenged he would 'take it for granted that neither the United States nor Great Britain are going to lift a finger to prevent the domination at the close of the war of most of Eastern and Southern Europe by the Soviet Union, and the imperialistic ambitions of the Soviet Union will be greatly accelerated and enhanced'. The Polish government-in-exile sought a return to the 1939 territorial boundaries whilst the USSR wanted to shift Poland's eastern border westwards to the River Oder and the so-called Curzon Line. Roosevelt secretly agreed to the Russian position but domestic considerations prevented him from making this public. He admitted to Stalin that he did not wish to lose the votes of 'six to seven million Americans of Polish extraction' in the 1944 election. The President was also unwilling to commit himself to a specific western boundary for Poland. In April 1943 he accepted the Soviet version of the Katyn Forest mass grave discovered close to Smolensk. Stalin claimed that the Nazis had murdered 12,500 Polish army officers and NCOs when even at the time there were strong suspicions that Soviet NKVD troops were responsible. The government of post-war Poland was a central issue at the Yalta Conference of February 1945. In July 1944 a Council of National

Liberation based at Lublin had been established by the Soviet Union and was widely seen as a move to dominate Poland through a puppet government. At Yalta Stalin agreed to a democratic broadening of the Lublin group and to hold 'free elections' in Poland. In return, America agreed to support the communist sponsored Lublin government. Roosevelt rejected Churchill's pleas for practical safeguards to ensure the outcome of 'free elections'. Genuine elections were never to take place. The Soviets accepted the Yalta agreement as a veiled American surrender of Poland and the Poles had every justification for feeling that they had been sold-out.

Roosevelt's wartime policies towards China are also open to charges of superficiality and naivety. The administration assured the American public that China was an important ally in the war against Japan. Jiang Jieshi, head of the Chinese Nationalist Government, was depicted as a strong leader who had rallied the long-suffering Chinese masses. However, support for Jiang consisted more of gestures than substantive action. For example, while the Chinese leader was made Supreme Commander of the United Powers in China, America extended relatively little material aid; Nationalist China received a mere 0.5 per cent of all Lend-Lease aid. There were many broken promises - the United States shipped less than 10 per cent of the aid which it had pledged to send and this was one factor in Jiang's ultimate defeat on the Chinese mainland by the communists led by Mao Ze Dong. The American President clung to the belief that a democratic and progressive China would emerge from the war. In fact, Jiang's regime was riddled with corruption and was dependent on regional warlords who ruthlessly exploited the Chinese peasantry. Few Americans understood the nature of the internal conflict in China and the administration's policies continued to seek unification of Nationalists and Communists by peaceful means. This was hopelessly unrealistic. General Stilwell, the Commander of the US forces in the China-Burma-India theatre of the war who had been appointed by Roosevelt, was an able soldier but a poor diplomat. A fundamental personality clash between Jiang and Stilwell did not smooth Sino-American relations. Frederick Marks, a historian critical of Roosevelt's policies, concluded that, 'His peculiar blend of action and inaction undermined Jiang even as it fell short of providing the basis for a positive relationship with Mao.'

Yet it was President Roosevelt's handling of the relationship with the Soviet Union that has provoked most criticism. The essence of the case against him is that he made promises that he could not keep and that he made too many concessions in the hope of gaining the co-operation of the Soviet Union in the post-war world whilst securing too little in return. The President had complete confidence in his ability to manage the relationship, writing to Churchill in March 1942, 'I think I can personally handle Stalin better than either your Foreign Office or my State Department. Stalin hates the guts of all your top people. He thinks he likes me better, and I hope he will continue to do so.' He dismissed a lengthy memorandum in 1942 which had been critical of the Soviets: 'I just have a hunch that Stalin is not that kind of man ... I think if I give him everything I possibly can and ask nothing in return, noblesse oblige - he won't try to annex anything and will work with me for a world of democracy and peace.' Roosevelt agreed $1 billion of supplies to the Soviet Union under Lend-Lease as early as November 1941. It was clearly a mistake and a rash move to promise Foreign Minister Molotov in June 1942 that a Second Front would be opened before the end of the year to alleviate pressure on Soviet forces. It was a promise which could not be kept. The US ambassador in Moscow warned shortly afterwards that, 'If such a front does not materialise quickly and on a large scale, these people will be so deluded in their belief in our sincerity of purpose ... that inestimable damage will be done.' As the ambassador had predicted, the delay of a Second Front until 1944 aroused Soviet anger and cynicism. One context of the US-Soviet relationship was that many Russians recalled that western nations had sought to strangle the Soviet Union at birth through their intervention in the Russian Civil War after 1918. The USSR must have suspected that the western Allies were dragging their feet whilst Russia bore the brunt of German armed might. It is worth contrasting the Soviet Union's loss of at least eight million military casualties and an estimated 16 million civilian deaths (possibly more) in the Second World War with the total loss of American lives of just over 400,000.

It was perhaps an awareness by Roosevelt of the enormous sacrifices being made by Soviet citizens, as well as a desire to keep the Soviet Union on board as a faithful present and future ally, that led to Roosevelt making so many concessions. Stalin gratefully received what was on offer and made only a few vague commitments in return. Historians have questioned whether the American President needed to offer so much at the Tehran Conference of November 1943 in return for the USSR's continued support against Germany and her pledge to join the war against Japan. He agreed to Soviet protection over Mongolia and acquisition of the Kurile Islands and the southern half of Sakhalin Island in the Western Pacific area. He also ceded Port Arthur to the USSR as a naval base on a long-term lease. The President seemed prepared to accept and even encourage Soviet advances in Europe and Asia without regard to the idealistic principles of political liberty to which the USSR as one of the 'United Nations' had pledged herself. Stalin promised a great deal at Tehran; religious liberty, the abolition of the Communist International committed to promoting world revolution, and a reformed Red Army. Grand words like this proved to be cheap and meaningless. Roosevelt may have been determined to avoid Woodrow Wilson's mistakes during and after the First World War of presenting too rigid and moralistic a position towards the communists but critics would argue that in his desire to be flexible and conciliatory

FDR went to the opposite extreme and was too soft in his negotiations with Stalin.

Roosevelt has appeared to some historians as too much the politician with an eye to the domestic scene and immediate prospects and too little the statesman. There had been an implied rebuke in Churchill's comment in September 1941 before the United States entered the war that 'nothing is more dangerous in wartime than to live in the temperamental atmosphere of a Gallup Poll, always feeling one's pulse and taking one's temperature'. In other words it was unwise to be over-influenced by the short-term swings of public opinion. Moreover, contemporary constitutional experts and more recent historians have seen the range of emergency presidential powers which Roosevelt took into his hands as dangerous. This concentration of the key diplomatic decisions into the hands of one man occurred at a time when his health, memory, and powers of concentration were declining. By the time of the Yalta Conference Roosevelt was a sick man. The lack of more formal policy-making structures was to have important implications when his successor Harry Truman assumed presidential powers unbriefed and only loosely aware of Roosevelt's thinking and objectives. Some of Roosevelt's decisions might be regarded as strategic errors. For example, his announcement at Casablanca in January 1943 that 'Unconditional Surrender' was the objective of the war against Germany and Japan has been condemned by scores of writers as one of the great mistakes of the war because it was likely to prolong German and Japanese resistance and their preparedness to fight to the end. He has been accused of lacking long-term vision - certainly subordinates found it difficult to keep his mind focused for long on any one problem. Few critics would deny Roosevelt's brilliant political skills, eloquence, and magnetic rhetoric but they would argue that it is easy to mistake form for substance.

3 FDR's Wartime Leadership: The Case for the Defence

In the House of Commons shortly after Roosevelt's death, Winston Churchill described him as a man of 'clear vision and vigour upon perplexing and complicated matters' and as 'the greatest champion of freedom who has ever brought help and comfort from the New World to the Old'. The President was the principal architect of the major strategic decisions governing the American war effort and these have withstood the test of time and the critical scrutiny of historians pretty well. Roosevelt's chief strategic concern was 'to defeat the Axis through the maximum possible use of American industrial power, but with the minimum possible expenditure of American lives'. This objective was achieved. The United States found itself involved in enormously complicated political questions as a result of wartime alliance; it could not have been otherwise given the extent of American commitments and resources throughout the world. Generally, Roosevelt picked his way sure-footedly through all sorts of potential political minefields. The 'Strange Alliance' of the Big Three held together. Britain, the world's greatest colonial power, the Soviet Union, the world's only communist state, and the United States, the world's greatest capitalist power led by a President who frequently criticised colonialism and was no friend of communism formed a successful Grand Alliance. Despite many stresses and strains the alliance held together to the end (although for a critical view see the cartoon by David Low on page 140). One of the ways in which Roosevelt sought to prevent bickering among the Allies was to keep war aims and the precise shape of the post-war settlement deliberately vague.

There were good reasons to postpone the opening of a Second Front in Europe and a cross-channel invasion launched from Britain despite the counter-claims of American military officers and Soviet leaders. Churchill was fearful of launching a premature invasion, tormented by visions of beaches 'choked with the flower of American and British youth' and 'tides running red with their blood'. The British were possibly accurate in predicting a bloodbath if 'Operation Sledgehammer' (the code-name for a limited cross-channel assault planned for 1942) was endorsed. Moreover, a failed cross-channel attack would have given no help to the Russians, exposed French supporters to Nazi vengeance, and further delayed the main operation. The President knew that such an attack could not be staged without British support. His endorsement of the North African campaign reflected both his concern for Anglo-American unity and a realisation that American morale required a quick and relatively safe involvement in the conflict for American troops as soon as possible. Harry Hopkins, a leading adviser, referred to the need to 'bloody' American forces.

It may be that political rather than military considerations were uppermost in Roosevelt's mind, but this is not necessarily grounds for criticism. With a Second Front possibly two years distant, Britain and the United States could not afford to leave the USSR as the only power militarily engaged against Germany. If American forces did not get into action against German forces pressure would build to concentrate on the Pacific War against Japan. Roosevelt was struggling against the formidable legacy of Pearl Harbor. The calls for revenge against Japan were intense; by contrast, American personnel and territory had scarcely been attacked by the Nazis with the effect that during 1942 opinion polls showed that up to 30 per cent of Americans inclined towards a compromise peace with Germany.

Defenders of Roosevelt would argue that whilst some of his wartime objectives were not achieved, his diplomatic leadership during the war represented the most effective expression of American interests and ideals that circumstances permitted. The military and practical realities resulting from the deployment or lack of availability of American armed forces often prevented alternative policies. Was it possible for the United States to 'get tough' with the USSR over Eastern Europe at a time when Russian influence was firmly established there? The Red Army's occupation of Eastern Europe severely limited Roosevelt's options. Was it possible for the United States to alter the political situation in China? A decision in 1943 to scrap plans for an invasion of Burma reflected both the American President's conviction by this stage that Jiang Jieshi was ineffective and independent-minded, and the limited power of the United States to influence events. Moreover, it is not surprising that China was hardly near the top of the American list of priorities. However much Americans disliked European colonialism, how could the United States force its allies to recognise the inevitability of independence in Asia? It is often said that politics is the art of the possible and Roosevelt was a master craftsman. Many decisions were dictated by military necessity. For example, Americans made temporary deals with some unsavoury right-wing leaders in French North Africa (Darlan) and Italy (Badaglio) to minimise casualties as they drove the Axis forces back. Pragmatism and the central aim of winning the war pushed some of the higher principles of the 'Declaration of the United Nations' into the background. It is important to underline the constraints within which Roosevelt was operating. It is unlikely that he could have significantly altered events in Europe or Asia after the war. Soviet expansion, Chinese strife, and colonial revolutions were largely beyond his power to prevent.

Arguably Roosevelt's policies towards the Soviet Union were realistic rather than naive and weak. From Pearl Harbor to Yalta the American President focused upon working together with Stalin against the common enemy and sought to bring about the defeat of the Axis powers in the shortest possible time. Roosevelt recognised that post-war stability required a Soviet-American accord and that Soviet power would then extend into Eastern Europe and parts of East Asia. His policies needed to be framed within these emerging realities.

The suggestion that FDR could have restrained Soviet expansion through greater realism or a tougher approach to Stalin is unpersuasive in the view of his defenders. A tough policy towards the USSR might well have jeopardised the successful prosecution of the war. Given the determination of the Soviet Union to extend its control westwards in order to create a 'buffer zone' to prevent future invasion and the vast area over-run by the Red Army, it is hard to see how any American President could have denied Russia its post-war domination of Eastern Europe. An all-out race to beat the Soviets to Berlin and Prague would have resulted in much higher allied casualties and an open-ended commitment to retain enormous occupation forces in Eastern Europe. The agreements made at the Yalta Conference were not seen as a disastrous sell-out at the time (see the cartoon on page 140). Indeed many of the compromises augured well for continued inter-allied co-operation. The immediate future of Germany was agreed and France was to join in the allied occupation, plans for the defeat of Japan were finalised, and there was a renewal of the Soviet pledge to enter the war against Japan three months after the German surrender. Stalin agreed to continue to deal with the Nationalists in China as the legitimate government and not to support the communists. There was endorsement of the new Soviet/Polish border and agreement on the establishment and the organisational framework of the United Nations. It was hoped that a restoration of the historic boundaries of Russia would be an incentive to get the Soviets to participate in the harmonious management of international relations envisaged at Tehran. Roosevelt did not give away much that he could have chosen not to give away. In February 1945 the atomic bomb was far from completion and it was judged that the promise of Soviet help against Japan (which was to be faithfully fulfilled) was worth the territorial concessions if it might shorten the war by months and save thousands of American lives. Moreover, it was not clear that an increase in Soviet influence in the Far East would necessarily harm American interests in that part of the world.

Roosevelt's appreciation of the importance of unity both on the homefront and between the Allies is easy to underestimate more than half a century later. He knew that effective action abroad required a reliable consensus at home and his election to an unprecedented fourth term of office in 1944 was a reflection of the American people's trust in his foreign policy and military judgements. His optimism was infectious. Time and again Roosevelt pushed for greater efforts, set higher goals, and acted with the 'jaunty conviction that people can do more than they think possible if they have to', as Warren Kimball has put it. He demonstrated active and inspirational leadership. The United States was involved in all the theatres of the war; in the Atlantic as well as the Pacific, in North Africa as well as South East Asia, in the Middle East as well as South America, and co-ordinating the various pieces of the military and diplomatic jigsaw was an enormous task. The Anglo-American relationship, despite its internal tensions and the cliched complaint of the British people that the 'Yanks' were 'oversexed, overpaid, overfed, and over here', was perhaps the most successful military alliance in history, sustained later in the war by the considerable diplomatic and military skills of General Dwight Eisenhower.

Roosevelt had been keen that the Combined Chiefs of Staff of the British and American armed forces establish a unified command. Roosevelt also believed that international stability could be achieved by strength and co-operation among the major powers. Support for a new international organisation increased steadily so that by early 1945 fully 90 per cent of the American people favoured inclusion in a world body. By championing the United Nations and building up a domestic consensus in its favour, Roosevelt avoided the fate of Woodrow Wilson's League of Nations proposals in 1919.

'Now Supposing We All Try To Go Somewhere Together', 7 August, 1942

'The Rock', Daily Herald, *13 February, 1945*

4 The War in the Far East: From Pearl Harbor to Hiroshima

The Japanese gambled with their surprise attack on Pearl Harbor that the American fleet could not be replaced in under a year, by which stage they would have consolidated their gains in the Pacific. The gamble nearly paid off. Early in 1942 country after country and island after island fell to a string of Japanese victories; these included the British possessions of Hong Kong, Malaya, and Singapore and the American administered territories of Guam and the Phillipines. By the summer of 1942 the Japanese were in Burma not far from India and had taken the Dutch East Indies. As Japanese forces advanced further into New Guinea, bombers attacked the Australian mainland. It seemed as if the power of the western nations in South East Asia had been broken. During the first months of fighting in the Pacific American servicemen were opposed by a better trained and equipped enemy. Defeat in the Phillipines was followed by the 'Bataan Death March' during which about 600 Americans died through dysentery, malaria, or starvation. By the end of 1942, however, the threat to Australia had been repulsed and it was clear that Japanese forces were over-extended. The scale of the mismatch between Japan and America in terms of production capacity and technological expertise was soon to become apparent. By early 1943 the United States began employing faster, more powerful fighter aircraft such as the P-38 Lightning and superior aircraft carriers and battleships in numbers the Japanese could not hope to match. The Pearl Harbor attack was not a knock-out blow. Most of the oil tanks, dry docks, and repair ships were unharmed. More importantly, America's aircraft carriers were at sea on manoeuvres in December 1941. Had America lost her aircraft carriers Japan's great gamble might have come off.

The United States had virtual autonomy in the Pacific and devoted nearly 40 per cent of its total war effort in the Second World War to the Pacific Theatre. The war has been described as the most complicated military endeavour in history. It was about twice as far from the United States to Asia as it was to Europe; in other words it took two ships going from the United States to Asia to do as much as one to Europe and shipping was in short supply. The strategy in the Pacific was to avoid Japanese strong points and initiate operations that would conserve men and materials. The war lasted as long as it did because the United States had to dislodge the enemy from defensive positions piecemeal rather than engage in massive battles where American strengths would have been decisive. American troops failed to get onto mainland Asia in significant numbers because America did not have enough manpower to carry on a large-scale land war in both Europe and Asia (China's vast manpower resources were not used effectively against Japan). The Americans planned a two-pronged advance. General Douglas

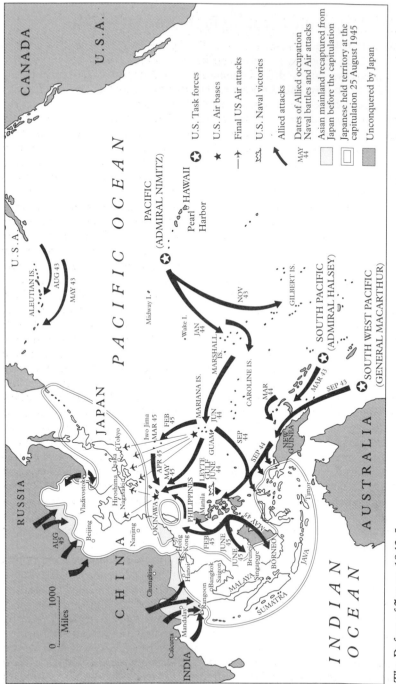

The Defeat of Japan 1943-5

MacArthur, who commanded American forces in the Far East, aimed to thrust upwards from the south-west Pacific through the Solomon Islands and New Guinea to the Phillipines. In the Central Pacific Admiral Chester Nimitz was to strike through the Marshall Islands, the Marianas, Iwo Jima, and Okinawa. An island-hopping campaign aimed to bring the army and the navy ever closer to the home islands of Japan and to capture secure bases for air attacks and invasion.

From the Battle of Midway in June 1942, when the United States shot down 300 Japanese aircraft and crippled 4 Japanese aircraft carriers, the Americans were on the offensive and the Japanese were in retreat (see the map on page 142). However, the following three years were not a story of uninterrupted American success and the casualties on both sides were horrific. Wherever allied forces advanced the Japanese fought back strongly, ready to die to the last man. American strategists learnt some bitter lessons as they underestimated the resilience of the Japanese and the ability of their fortifications to survive naval and air attacks. There were some key turning-point victories for the Americans. In June 1944, for example, the Battle of the Phillipine Sea became known informally as 'The Great Marianas Turkey Shoot'. In one day Japanese naval airpower was virtually destroyed as American planes shot down hundreds of poorly armed Japanese aircraft, many of which were piloted by novices, like turkeys. America had 900 carrier-based aircraft - twice the number of the Japanese - and only suffered light losses. Later in the same day the remaining Japanese carrier force was badly damaged and the strategically important islands of Saipan and Tinian fell to the Americans without interference from the Japanese navy. By October 1944 US forces were back on the Phillipines and General MacArthur had returned as he had promised. This touched off the Battle for Leyte Gulf, the largest naval battle in history. Four Japanese fleets met two American fleets and the Imperial Japanese Navy came off worse suffering heavy losses. When they lost the Phillipines (American forces entered Manila in February 1945) the Japanese had effectively lost the war because the supply routes carrying raw materials for Japanese industry were lost. In particular Japan lacked oil resources. Home production was little more than a tenth of minimum needs and the rest had to come across the seas. Of what was produced in the oilfields of Southern Asia the following percentages reached Japan: in 1942, 40 per cent; in 1943, 15 per cent; in 1944, 5 per cent; in 1945, none. Japanese ships, aircraft, tanks, and vehicles were all virtually eliminated. They had no fuel.

However, completely subduing Japan represented no easy task. The Japanese resistance at Iwo Jima, an eight mile square island of mainly volcanic rock, was typical. American forces inched forward against Japanese forces unprepared to surrender. Surrender went against the ancient Samurai code of honour. Of 21,000 Japanese troops only 200 were taken alive. Nearly 7,000 US Marines were killed and 20,000 were wounded. A fanatical patriotic loyalty to their nation and emperor had been inculcated in the Japanese soldiers. Many soldiers and civilians chose suicide rather than surrender. At Okinawa, only 350 miles from the Japanese mainland, the 100,000 strong Japanese army, outnumbered by 2:1, again made the Americans pay in blood for every foot of soil. Between April and June 1945, 2,000 'Kamikaze' pilots destroyed 30 US warships and damaged 200 more. About 5,000 men from the US Navy were killed and an equal number were wounded. Nearly 8,000 of the American ground forces died with more than 30,000 wounded. Only 7,000 Japanese soldiers survived. Japan's inner defences had been breached by the spring of 1945 and the home islands lay wide open to attack from the air. There was a systematic razing of Japan's mainly wooden cities. In one such raid on Tokyo over 16 square miles of the city were flattened and 70,000 civilians perished. Japan was desperately short of resources and raw materials such as oil, iron and steel, and food. Starvation hovered close as the rice crop failed. Still the Japanese prepared to defend their homeland and refused to surrender.

This was the context in which Truman was informed of the existence of a new and powerful weapon shortly after assuming the presidency. Truman inherited the assumption from Roosevelt that the atomic bomb was a legitimate weapon to end the war. No American policy maker ever effectively challenged this assumption. The Manhattan Project under the direction of Dr Robert Oppenheimer began in 1939 with the sole purpose of harnessing the energy of the atom to produce a bomb that could be carried by aircraft. Churchill later wrote that 'the decision whether or not to use the atomic bomb to compel the surrender of Japan was never even an issue'. For American leaders and citizens there were few moral constraints on what weapons were acceptable in war. The firebombings of Tokyo and other Japanese cities had produced few cries of outrage in the United States. Few Americans were troubled by the mass killing of enemy citizens, especially if they were yellow-skinned (the racial factor in the decision to use the bomb cannot be ignored - later experts questioned whether the United States would have used it against the white people of Berlin). There was a desire for revenge against Japan. President Truman hinted at this in a private letter in mid-August 1945: 'Nobody is more disturbed over the use of atomic bombs than I am but I was greatly disturbed over the unwarranted attack by the Japanese on Pearl Harbor. The only language they seem to understand is the one we have been using to bombard them. When you deal with a beast you have to treat him as a beast. It is most regrettable but nevertheless true.' The first atomic bomb was dropped on the Japanese city of Hiroshima on 6 August 1945 from the American plane 'Enola Gay'. Over 70,000 people died immediately and another 70,000 were injured. 97 per cent of the city's buildings were damaged or destroyed. Two days later a second bomb was dropped on Nagasaki killing 60,000.

There have been many subsequent criticisms of the combat use of the atomic bomb. It has been argued that the bombs were not necessary to end the war and that the American administration knew this. American leaders knew that Japan was on the verge of defeat and therefore close to surrender. Some historians have argued that the dropping of the bombs had the secondary purpose of keeping Russia out of the East Asian post-war settlement. Secretary of War Henry Stimson admitted that it was American policy 'to wear this weapon rather ostentatiously on our hip'. There was perhaps a desire to impress the Russians with the power of the bomb and thereby deter Soviet European expansion. The timing of events supports this interpretation (Truman casually informed Stalin that the United States had a 'new weapon' at the Potsdam Conference in July 1945 and was pleased, though surprised and even confused, when the Soviet leader did not press for details). The Americans expected the USSR to enter the war on or about the 8 August (and indeed the Soviets invaded Manchuria and Korea precisely on schedule) but the first bomb was dropped on 6 August. The US administration appeared to be in a hurry. America had no major military operations planned before 1 November 1945. They might have awaited the effects of the Russian declaration of war on Japan or pursued a political solution to end the war as a new Japanese cabinet put out peace feelers. Other alternatives were to demonstrate the power of the atomic bomb or to modify the surrender terms required of Japan. It is clear that the Japanese cabinet was looking for an honourable peace. They sent messages to the USSR hoping that they would act as intermediaries which American code breakers intercepted. They wanted guarantees that Emperor Hirohito would not lose his position. Privately the Allies had agreed at Potsdam that the Emperor could remain as a constitutional monarch in Japan but the terms of the 'Potsdam Declaration', Truman's final ultimatum to the Japanese, did not offer them this concession. Truman decided on the dropping of the bomb without warning.

The simplest explanation of Truman's decision is perhaps the most convincing. He ordered the use of the atomic bomb against Japanese civilians primarily to end the war quickly and save American lives. The President later wrote: 'The final decision of where and when to use the atomic bomb was up to me. Let there be no mistake about it. I regarded the bomb as a military weapon and never had any doubt that it should be used.' Although Japan had clearly lost the war she was far from crushed. She still retained control of much of China, most of south-east Asia, and all of Korea and Manchuria. The Japanese army was more or less intact and the air force was a major threat. The army was estimated at up to two million men in Manchuria, and there were some 5,350 'Kamikaze' planes ready for use and 7,000 more in storage. An American invasion of the Japanese home islands would have been a bloody affair. Having said this, it is undeniable that the bomb represented a considerable diplomatic bonus that American leaders believed would enhance American bargaining power in the emerging Cold War with the Soviet Union. The combination of the Hiroshima and Nagasaki bombs and the Soviet declaration of war prompted Emperor Hirohito to end the war. 500 Japanese military officers committed ritual suicide. The Japanese surrender was received on board the USS Missouri on 2 September 1945.

5 The USA in 1945: The Emergence of a Superpower and Early Cold War Skirmishes

The end of the war left the United States by far the wealthiest and most powerful nation-state in the world. In the four years from December 1941 to September 1945 America had been able to fight a two-ocean war as well as to finance a substantial part of the war effort of its two main Allies, Britain and the Soviet Union. The war had not left the United States bankrupt or destroyed its economy as it had those of the other major powers. Germany's bid for mastery in Europe had collapsed as had Japan's bid in the Far East and Pacific. Britain had lost a quarter of its national wealth and was transformed from the world's second largest creditor nation to its greatest debtor. France had been occupied and never again achieved great power status. The United States had needed little or no rationing or restriction of domestic consumption - during the war the country sustained a consumer goods boom on an unprecedented scale. America's Gross National Product rose from $88.6 billion in 1939 to $135 billion in 1945 stimulated by the vast surge in war expenditure. The United States gold reserves of $20 billion at the end of the war represented almost two-thirds of the world's total of $33 billion. Immediately after the war more than half of the total manufacturing production of the world took place within the USA. Moreover, by 1945 not only did the American economy dwarf all others, but American economic principles had been institutionalised in a series of international monetary agencies such as the International Monetary Fund (IMF) and the World Bank. The IMF was to assist nations in overcoming balance of payments problems through short-term loans and 36 per cent of the Fund's original $8.8 billion resources were provided by the United States. America's economic dominance in 1945 was overwhelming and in some ways artificial but many of the gains were permanent.

The Second World War marked the transition of the United States from a major world power to a superpower and also accelerated that process. Economic power was reflected in military strength. During the war the United States developed the institutions and capabilities of a superpower. In May 1940 the United States army was only the nineteenth largest in the world; it was widely scattered across the nation and was poorly equipped with out-dated tanks and planes. To defeat the Axis, the United States constructed a two-ocean navy and drafted, trained, and serviced huge armed forces which totalled some 12.1 million by May 1945. The development of the US Navy and Army Air Forces linked to a network of American military bases, for example on Pacific and Atlantic islands, gave the United States increased mobility of power for influencing and responding to a greatly changed world order. The navy possessed a fleet of 1,200 major warships; in both carrier task forces and its Marine corps divisions the United States had clearly shown its ability to project its power across the globe to any region accessible from the sea. Command of the air was seen as the guarantor of American security in the atomic age (at a time when America had a monopoly of nuclear weapons for the foreseeable future); more than 2,000 heavy bombers and 1,000 ultra-long range B-29s provided this command. America was in an extraordinarily favourable strategic position. There was an inevitable and considerable scaling down of American military resources as the war ended and domestic opinion pressed for retrenchment and lower taxation. Nevertheless, although there was considerable physical withdrawal, Americans found their informal influence in various lands around the globe hardening into something more formal. The contraction of Anglo-French power and that of the Axis left a vacuum for the United States to fill, sharing, for example, in the occupation of Germany, dominating post-war Japan, and projecting its influence into China and the Middle East.

In addition to her enormous economic and military strength America had also gained a great deal of political prestige from the war both at home and overseas. The United States had provided the tools and men to save Europe and Russia from Hitler and the Nazis. The American consciousness was imprinted with images of overwhelming US military successes. The war in the Pacific was, according to popular culture, won by the US Navy and Marine Corps, whilst the Normandy invasion not only turned the tide against Hitler, but was presented as an American show. American Allies sometimes showed bitterness in private at these inaccurate stereotypes. The British foreign minister Anthony Eden wrote in 1944: 'Americans have a much exaggerated conception of the military contribution they are making in this war. They lie freely about this e.g. figures of percentages of forces for Overlord or their share of sunken U-Boats and we are too polite'. But Churchill was happy to fuel the war-inspired visions of American omnipotence, informing the House of Commons in July 1944 that the Ardennes campaign was 'the greatest American battle of the war and will, I believe, be regarded as an ever-famous American victory'. In political circles the Second World War prompted American leaders and the US Congress to conclude that they had to use the nation's strength to protect and advance its interests. This represented a dramatic change in the way that the United States thought of its interests and ideals and its involvement in the world around it. There was, as one historian has put it 'an enhanced awareness of its global reach and a new conviction that its own self-interest required a greater managerial role in world affairs'. Prior to the war the dominant view among policy-makers had been that the security of the United States required little more than insulating the Western hemisphere from outside influences. A lesson absorbed from the Fall of France in 1940 and the Japanese attack on Pearl Harbor was that one of America's main interests was to keep Europe and Asia free from control by a single potentially hostile power.

The more extended outlook of American foreign policy was reflected in a Navy Day speech made by President Harry Truman in New York on 27 October 1945 about American power and principles. He stated that, 'The foreign policy of the United States is based firmly on fundamental principles of righteousness and justice. In carrying out those principles we shall firmly adhere to what we believe to be right; and we shall not give our approval to any compromises with evil.' He outlined 12 fundamental principles including:

1 2. We believe in the eventual return of sovereign rights and self-government to all peoples who have been deprived of them by force.
3. We shall approve no territorial changes in any friendly part of the
5 world unless they accord with the freely expressed wishes of the people concerned.
4. We believe that all peoples who are prepared for self-government should be permitted to choose their own form of government by their own freely expressed choice, without
10 interference from any foreign source. That is true in Europe, in Asia, in Africa, as well as in the Western hemisphere ...
6. We shall refuse to recognise any government imposed upon any nation by the force of any foreign power. In some cases it may be impossible to prevent forceful imposition of such a government.
15 But the United States will not recognise any such government.

The other principles outlined were: a denial of any American desire for territorial expansion, a desire to help Germany and Japan establish peaceful democratic government, freedom of the seas, fair trading arrangements, good neighbour principles in the Western hemisphere, economic collaboration between nations, freedom of expression and religion, and support for the United Nations. Under Roosevelt's subtle persuasion, Americans came to see a more internationalist approach as the best way to avoid another war. By 1947 President Truman could proclaim a 'doctrine' that would legitimise American intervention in any part of the world and committed America to enforce the principles that he had outlined in 1945: 'I believe that it must be the policy of the United States to support free peoples who are resisting attempted subjugation by armed minorities or by outside pressures.'

Truman's words need to be understood in the context of an emerging 'Cold War' with the Soviet Union. A full analysis of the escalating tensions between the United States and the Soviet Union in the years and decades following the Second World War lies beyond the scope of this book but even by the end of 1945 it was clear that hopes of continuing the wartime alliance had foundered and that there was a gulf of mistrust and hostility between the two countries. The Yalta Conference represented the high point of allied diplomacy and unity. The events which helped so quickly bring about the breakdown of the Yalta accords are complex. Many issues played their role: political arrangements in Poland and Eastern Europe generally, the four power division of Germany and the question of reparations, the Soviet request for American aid, the emerging civil war in China, the setting up of the United Nations, and the American monopoly of atomic power. Roosevelt was concerned during the last months of his life about the increasing frequency of misunderstandings with the Russians but at no point sought to contest the substantial expansion of Soviet influence in Europe and Asia that the end of the war would bring. Rather, he hoped to maintain a balance of power by convincing Russians that security could best be attained through co-operation rather than unilateral efforts. Following Roosevelt's death in April 1945, United States policy-makers increasingly read the USSR as a bullying aggressor bent on grabbing territory, subduing neighbours, and disturbing the post-war peace through subversion. One of Truman's 'hawkish' advisers was Averell Harriman, US ambassador to Moscow. He warned Truman at an important early meeting of all his key advisers on 20 April 1945 that America was faced with a 'barbarian invasion of Europe', that Soviet control over any foreign country represented the extension of the Soviet system with secret police, extinction of freedom of speech etc., 'and that we had to decide what should be our attitude in the face of these unpleasant facts'. He called for 'the abandonment of the illusion that for the immediate future the Soviet Government was going to act in accordance with the principles which the rest of the world held to in international affairs'.

There is no doubt that Truman brought a tougher tone to American policies towards the Soviet Union, although he was keen faithfully to follow the course set out by his predecessor. The former Missouri senator had been a late and surprise choice as Roosevelt's vice-president. Truman was a comparative innocent in terms of foreign policy with no direct experience in the conduct of foreign affairs, and he had been generally ignored by Roosevelt in the three months after his inaugural speech. This increased the influence of hard-line advisers such as Harriman, James Byrnes, soon to be Truman's Secretary of State, and George Kennan, a leading state department official in Moscow. Truman assumed the presidency at a crucial and delicate time; by April 1945 it was clear that Stalin was not keeping his promises over Poland. Truman was clear that the USSR would need American economic aid to reconstruct their country (in January 1945 Stalin requested a $6 billion loan). American post-war policy was based in part on the belief that no matter what the United States said or did, the Russians could not protest because they had to have American money. This view turned out to be mistaken. At another important meeting with advisers on 23 April 1945 Truman stated that 'Our agreements with the Soviet Union have so far been a one-way street and that this can not continue.' Later the same day he gave the Russian Foreign Minister Molotov a severe dressing-down in none too diplomatic language. When Molotov complained 'I have never been talked to like that in my life', Truman replied 'Carry out your agreements and you won't get talked to like that.' Nevertheless, Truman did not want a break with the Soviet Union at this stage and was keen to get Stalin's commitment to join the war against Japan. This had the potential to save hundreds of thousands of American casualties. The Potsdam Conference in the east of Germany in July 1945 slightly softened his attitude. He recorded his initial impressions of Stalin in his diary, over optimistically as events turned out, 'He is straightforward, knows what he wants and will compromise when he can't get it ... I can deal with Stalin. He is honest - but smart as hell'. He wrote to his wife on 18 July 'I've gotten what I came for. Stalin goes to war with no strings on it ... I'll say that we'll end the war a year sooner now and think of the kids that won't get killed. That is the important thing.'

Nevertheless, the US-Soviet relationship continued to deteriorate. There has been considerable debate amongst historians about the reasons for such a rapid sharpening of antagonisms and about whether one side or the other deserves to be allocated more of the blame. The orthodox western view is that the Soviet Union was entirely responsible for the breakdown because it had swallowed up extra territories during the war itself (the Baltic States, parts of Finland, Romania, and Eastern Czechoslovakia), and then taken advantage of its military strength in Eastern Europe after the war to overthrow democratic government and install communist puppet regimes. There is no doubt that the Soviets acted ruthlessly in Eastern Europe at the end of the war. For example, the eastern zone of Germany was unceremoniously stripped of its industrial resources. Churchill, in his famous 'Iron Curtain' speech of March 1946 saw Soviet actions as a prelude to a bid to dominate the whole of Europe. The Soviets sponsored strong communist movements in France and Italy where it was by no means impossible that the communists would capture power; in both countries communists had been outstandingly effective in wartime resistance movements and economic and social breakdown was an increasingly imminent possibility. The orthodox view would tend to emphasise the significance of Marxist-Leninist ideology with its insistence upon encouraging

World Revolution, and would depict Stalin as keen to enlarge the number of communist-dominated countries controlled from Moscow. In the Middle East, for example, Soviet troops remained in the north of Iran and tried to sponsor a breakaway movement to bring the area under Soviet control. The USSR was also expanding in East Asia as a result of Allied concessions at Yalta. It is unsurprising that fears relating to Soviet expansion were so extensive in 1945 and subsequent years. By 1949 the western boundary of the expanding Russian Empire was now advanced to a line 80 per cent of the way from Russia's pre-war boundaries to the boundaries of Holland, Belgium, and France.

A revisionist view, which became popular in the 1960s and 1970s, was that American policies also played a significant part in provoking the Cold War. It was argued that the United States was insufficiently sensitive to genuine and legitimate Soviet concerns about security. Russian history gave her a deep fear of the outside world. Russia lacked defensible western boundaries and had suffered 10 centuries of devastation by invaders. With mountains and impassable waters lacking, sheer space had to make do in their stead. Stalin commented to Harry Hopkins, who went to Moscow as an envoy in May 1945, 'Twice in the last thirty years our enemies the Germans have passed through this corridor. It is in Russia's interests that Poland should be strong and powerful, in a position to shut the door ... by her own force'. As regards Soviet security concerns, the United States appeared to be operating double standards. In practice the United States maintained considerable control over Central and South America which it regarded as its backyard (through the support of military dictatorships in most cases). If it was true that free elections in eastern Europe would result in anti-Soviet governments, it was equally true that free elections in Latin America would probably bring to power anti-American governments. Moreover, there was a case for arguing that Americans had used the atomic bomb in August 1945 in part to impress and threaten Russia. Stalin was acutely aware of Russian vulnerability to capitalism's new weapon, whose existence had been kept from Russia, and whose secrets of manufacture the United States announced she intended to preserve as a 'sacred trust'. Soviet President Kalinin commented at the end of the war, 'Even now after the greatest victory known to history we cannot for one moment forget ... that our country remains the one socialist state in the world ... Only the ... most immediate danger which threatened us from Germany has disappeared'. The American occupation of Japan and the growth of US Pacific bases increased the Russian fear of encirclement.

Recent interpretations of the origins of the Cold War underline the conflict between capitalism and communism and the inevitable distrust and competition when two irreconcilable ideologies clashed. In this light the years 1941-5 can be seen as a fleeting and temporary truce. The US administration deliberately took a long time to consider the Soviet request for credit in January 1945, ended Lend-Lease abruptly, and refused to grant reparations out of German production in the amounts necessary for the rebuilding of the destroyed Soviet Union. Revisionist historians placed less emphasis on Soviet expansionism than on the world-wide expansion of American capitalism. Certainly the United States had made considerable economic gains at Britain's expense, and American policy makers attempted to use this enhanced economic influence to create an environment within which American businesses could operate without restrictions all over the world. An 'Open Door' for American commercial interests in Eastern Europe would have meant a capitalist and hostile threat on the Soviet doorstep. From the perspective of Moscow the Americans were engaged in aggressive atomic diplomacy and dollar diplomacy. With new archives becoming available in the USSR and Eastern Europe, and with the end of the Cold War allowing historians to look at the whole conflict in a new light, the historiography of the rapid breakdown in US-Soviet relations at the end of the Second World War is likely to undergo further significant reinterpretation over the coming years.

What is clear is that by the end of 1945 President Truman's patience with the Soviet failure to keep their promises and continuing territorial expansion had run out. He drafted the following letter to Secretary of State Byrnes and, according to Truman's memoirs, he read it aloud to him in the Oval Office on 5 January 1946:

1 At Potsdam we were faced with an accomplished fact and were by
   circumstances almost forced to agree to Russian occupation of
   eastern Poland, and that part of Germany east of the Oder river by
   Poland. It was a high-handed outrage. There isn't a doubt in my
5 mind that Russia intends an invasion of Turkey and the seizure of
   the Black Sea Straits to the Mediterranean. Unless Russia is faced
   with an iron fist and strong language, another war is in the making.
   Only one language do they understand - 'How many divisions have
   you?' I do not think we should play compromise any longer. We
10 should refuse to recognise Romania and Bulgaria until they comply
   with our requirements; we should let our position on Iran be
   known in no uncertain terms ... and we should maintain complete
   control of Japan and the Pacific. We should rehabilitate China and
   create a strong central government there. We should do the same
15 for Korea. Then we should insist on the return of our ships from
   Russia and force a settlement of the Lend-Lease debt of Russia.
   I'm tired of babying the Soviets.

Truman later described this letter as 'the point of departure of our policy'. The entire memorandum with its sweeping geographical references and its grandiose strategic ambitions was couched in the vocabulary of a permanent American overseas commitment and an unending military expenditure.

Truman's letter was also the product of a sense of frustration that America's awesome power in 1945 could not be brought to bear. The hope expressed by Byrnes in June 1945 that American possession of the atomic bomb 'would make Russia more manageable in Europe' proved unfulfilled. However great America's economic and military power, there were limits to the extent that even the most powerful nation could project its influence beyond its borders. No troops ever set forth on a crusade to liberate Poland. The United States could not block Soviet expansion. American influence would never be as great as American power. Over the next three decades American leaders and the American people were forced to learn that bitter lesson in Eastern Europe, Korea, Vietnam, and other parts of the world. Nevertheless, the advice of America's founding fathers to avoid 'entangling alliances' appeared by 1945 to have been set aside. The British Prime Minister Clement Attlee commented at a White House dinner in November 1945,

1 The discoveries of science are transcending seas and transcending oceans. We must not let anything rob us of our freedom and of our democracy. Rather, we must try to see whether we cannot give to all nations that kind of security in which through long years on
5 both sides of the Atlantic we worked up in practice.

By 1948 Congress was to confirm the European Recovery Programme (Marshall Aid) and enter into discussions which were to lead, the following year, to the signature of a permanent 'entangling alliance' the North Atlantic Treaty Organisation. America's relationship with the rest of the world had changed dramatically from the isolationism which had impelled Congress to reject American membership of the League of Nations at the end of the First World War and the cautious non-interventionism of the 1930s. America stepped forwards, perhaps over-confidently, to assume the responsibilities of world leadership. The lessons of the inter-war years were still fresh. As Truman put it in 1948:

1 After the First World War the United States had its first great opportunity to lead the world to peace. I have always believed that it was the will of God at that time that we should enter into and lead the League of Nations. How much misery and suffering the
5 world would have been spared if we had followed Woodrow Wilson. We are not making the same mistake this time that we made in 1920. God willing, we will not ever make that mistake again.

Making notes on 'The USA and the Second World War'

The emphasis of this chapter is less upon the military detail of Second World War than on broader diplomatic questions relating to, 1 American war aims; 2 The relationship with wartime Allies (Britain and the Soviet Union); 3 Why America won the Pacific War; and, 4 The early origins of the Cold War. Central to most of these questions are the actions and thinking of President Roosevelt. Your notes need to be organised to enable you to throw as much light as possible on these areas.

Use the second and third sections of this chapter to draw up a balance sheet of things that can be said in favour of Roosevelt's leadership of the American war effort and criticisms of his handling of international relations. A similarly useful task might be to construct a balance sheet of agreement and disagreement between the Allies at their various wartime conferences. On what issues was there unity? What divided the leaders of the 'Big Three'?

In your consideration of the war in the Pacific between December 1941 and August 1945 you will again find it useful to construct a timeline of key events to establish a clear chronology in your mind. What were the difficulties facing the United States in conducting war in East Asia? Why was it so difficult to overcome Japanese resistance after they had begun to retreat? When you come to consider the decision to drop the atomic bomb, you might find that the most fruitful way of consolidating your knowledge and understanding is to participate in a classroom debate on the question, 'Was President Truman justified in his decision to drop atomic bombs on the Japanese cities of Hiroshima and Nagasaki?' Prepare the arguments for and against this motion. Try to argue as far as possible from the perspective of the situation in August 1945 rather than the perspective of the late 1990s.

The final section of this chapter demonstrates the extent of American global influence in 1945. What are the defining characteristics of a 'superpower'? Consideration is given to the rapid deterioration in the US-Soviet relationship in 1945. How much blame do you attach to Roosevelt and Truman for the breakdown in relations? How sympathetic a view do you take of Stalin's actions in Eastern Europe in 1944-5? There are no easy answers here, but you do need to be able to marshall the arguments and evidence on each side and to reach your own conclusions.

Answering essay questions on 'The USA and The Second World War'

There are four main areas where examiners are most likely to focus their attention on this topic. The four areas are, Roosevelt's leadership, American war aims, the dropping of the atomic bomb, and the start of

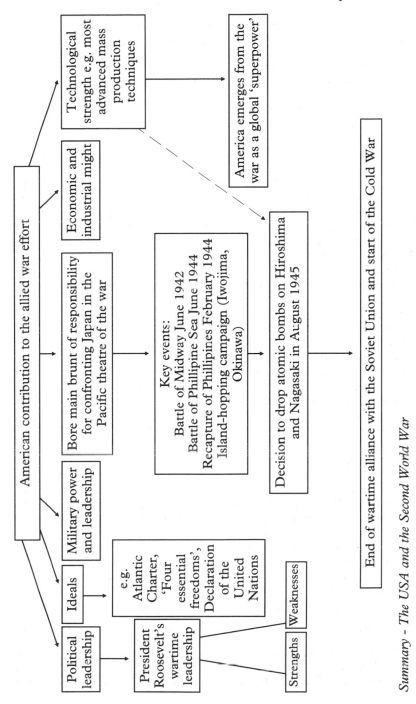

Summary – The USA and the Second World War

the Cold War. The following questions are typical:

1   Assess FDR's role as a war leader between 1941 and 1945.
2   How great a war leader was FDR?
3   Analyse the war aims of the USA between 1941 and the Potsdam Conference of 1945.
4   'There was little military justification for the decision to drop an atomic bomb on Hiroshima'. How far do you agree with this statement?
5   Had the Cold War begun by the time that the Potsdam Conference ended?
6   To what extent was the USA responsible for the start of the Cold War?

Questions 1 and 2 are similar but not quite the same. In both answers you will need to identify the characteristics of strong leadership, demonstrate an understanding of Roosevelt's main wartime objectives, and reach a judgement on how well the American President measured up to the demands placed upon him. However, there are subtle differences between the questions which you need to be alive to. Question 1 is more difficult; the wording gives you less structure to get your teeth into. What is meant by role? Does this mean looking at Roosevelt's managerial and decision-making style? You certainly need to explore his relationship with Winston Churchill and Joseph Stalin. You also need to look at the domestic audience which Roosevelt always had to keep in mind. The word 'assess' does not mean ramble on about - there is a need for critical evaluation. Question 2 lends itself more easily to a 'on the one hand . . . on the other hand' approach where you can balance Roosevelt's strengths and weaknesses and come down on one side or the other. You should ask yourself what are the criteria for judging 'greatness'.

Question 3 is by no means easy. There is a danger that a question like this can lead to a narrative answer which describes American involvement in the war between 1941 and 1945 with little or no sense of focus. Can you make a distinction between long-term and short-term aims? Should you break the question down into military, political, and economic war aims? Did Roosevelt have clear war aims at all? What disagreement was there about what the United States was trying to achieve? It is important to remember that aims can change in the light of changing circumstances. Moreover, American war aims were by no means always compatible with those of her Allies.

Questions 4 to 6 all cover highly contentious ground where there is little consensus among historians. A good way of establishing where you feel that you stand is to try to write a succinct eight to ten line conclusion on each of the questions. Ironically, the conclusion is sometimes the best place to start! The arguments relating to the dropping of the atomic bomb and the start of the Cold War are rehearsed in the text. You need to marshal your analysis and supporting evidence as powerfully as you can, always remembering to acknowledge and address opposing arguments. Question 5 is particularly difficult to reach a verdict on. Amongst the questions that you need to ask are: Did the Cold War in reality begin in 1917? What are the other key turning points at which it could be claimed that the Cold War started? (Yalta, the death of Roosevelt, Truman's showdown with Molotov, Hiroshima, the end of Lend-Lease, and Churchill's Iron Curtain speech all have alternative claims to Potsdam.) What part did the Potsdam Conference play in accelerating US - Soviet antagonism? You are also advised to consult the companion volume in this series The USA and The Cold War for further insights. The focus of attention in this chapter has been restricted to those origins of the Cold War which lay in America's wartime relationship with the Soviet Union.

You will see from the four guidance sections on essay-writing skills in this book that there are a range of strategies open to you in planning and writing good answers. One final point is worth underlining; excepting the small minorities of extremely able and talented students at the top and of weak and underprepared students at the bottom, most students will enter the examination hall with a roughly similar amount of understanding and knowledge in their heads. There is a bunching of most students somewhere in the middle. This is good news - it can mean that a small improvement of two or three marks for each answer can yield a disproportionate gain and boost a middling grade to a good one. This underlines the importance of a well-honed essay-writing technique. Not all students will be able to package their understanding and demonstrate their knowledge with the same degree of clarity. Sustained practice at writing snappy and immediate introductions, formulating crisp and well-rounded conclusions, and dividing up material thematically into manageable paragraphs can have a positive pay-off. If you can ally these skills to a flexibility in your thinking which will allow you to respond to the particular challenge set by the examiner rather than falling back on a Blue Peter style of essay-writing (i.e. 'here's one I prepared earlier'), your hard work should receive the reward it deserves. Good luck!

Answering source-based questions on '*The USA and the Second World War*'

1 President Roosevelt and the Wartime Alliance
Study the two cartoons on page 140.
a) What is the message of the British cartoonist David Low in the cartoon published in August 1942? (You should comment on the drivers, what is written about the contents of the truck, and the caption). (6 marks)

b) What actions had President Roosevelt undertaken to co-ordinate allied strategy by August 1942? (5 marks)
c) What impression is the cartoonist seeking to convey about the Yalta conference in 'The Rock'. (4 marks)
d) Did the conference achieve 'Complete Agreement' as far as Roosevelt was concerned? (5 marks)

2 The Defeat of Japan
Look at the map on page 142 and the relevant section of text.
a) From what base did America launch its naval and air attacks upon Japan? (1 mark)
b) How much territory did Japan still hold before the decision to drop atomic bombs on Hiroshima and Nagasaki? (4 marks)
c) How useful is this map in helping you to assess the problems which the United States faced in defeating Japan? (10 marks)

3 President Truman's views on foreign policy and Soviet expansionism
Read the extracts from Truman's Navy Day speech in October 1945 (page 148) and the letter to Secretary of State, James Byrnes which he drafted in January 1946 (page 152).
a) Look at the fourth principle outlined by Truman in his speech in October 1945. Explain what he meant by this. (4 marks)
b) Compare the two extracts. Account for the differences between them in terms of their language and tone. (5 marks)
c) What were the detailed reasons for the American leader losing patience with the Soviet Union by January 1946. (4 marks)
d) To what extent had America been 'babying the Soviets' in 1945? (7 marks)

Chronological Table

1917	January	Germany resumed unrestricted submarine warfare
	February	Zimmerman Telegram
	April	America entered into the First World War
1918	January	President Wilson's Fourteen Points speech
	May	Significant numbers of US troops began to arrive in Europe
	November	German surrender based on the terms of the Fourteen Points
1919	Jan.-June	Versailles Peace Conference
	July	The Treaty Fight in the American Senate. America rejected
1920	February	Membership of the League of Nations
	November	Landslide victory for the Republican candidate, Warren Harding, in the Presidential election
1920s		Republican commitment under Presidents Harding, Coolidge, and Hoover to political isolationism
1921-22		Washington Conference agreements with Japan
1924		Dawes Plan helped to re-organize German reparations payments (Later further reduced under the Young Plan of 1929)
1928	August	Kellogg-Briand Pact agreed
1929	October	Wall Street Crash triggered global economic recession
1931	September	Manchurian Crisis triggered by the Mukden incident
1933	March	President Roosevelt announced his 'Good Neighbour' policy with respect to Latin America
1933-38		Roosevelt worried about Nazi and Japanese expansionism but went with the tide of isolationist sentiment and focused upon domestic priorities
	June-July	Failure of International Economic Conference in London
1933		Diplomatic recognition accorded to the Soviet Union
1934-36		Nye Committee investigations into the armaments industry
1935-37		Enactment of Neutrality Laws
1936	November	Roosevelt re-elected in an electoral landslide
1937	August	Roosevelt made his 'Quarantine' speech
	October	Failure of Brussels Conference to resolve conflict between China and Japan

1938	December	Declaration of Lima
1939	January	Roosevelt called for all 'methods short of war' to deter aggression in his annual message to Congress
1939-41		Roosevelt edged America closer to Britain, France, and China but America stayed out of the Second World War
1940	September	Destroyers for Bases deal agreed with Britain
	September	The America First Committee established
	November	Roosevelt again re-elected
1941	March	Lend-Lease Plan agreed by Congress
	June	Lend-Lease aid extended to the Soviet Union
	July	Economic sanctions against Japan were hardened after the occupation of Indo-China
	August	Declaration of the Atlantic Charter
	December	Pearl Harbor
1941-45		America made a substantial military and economic contribution to allied victory in the Second World War in both the Pacific and European theatres
1945	February	Yalta Conference
	April	Death of Roosevelt. Succeeded by his Vice-President, Harry Truman
	July	Potsdam Conference
	August	Atomic bombs dropped on Japanese cities of Hiroshima and Nagasaki
1945-46		The Start of the Cold War

Further Reading

The best recent textbook on the period covered by this volume is: **Akira Iriye**, *The Globalising of America 1913-1945* (CUP, 1993) This is succinct, well-written, and full of thought-provoking ideas. It also contains an excellent bibliographical essay.

Another clear survey of the themes and events addressed in this book is a collaborative textbook: **Thomas G. Paterson, J. Garry Clifford, Kenneth Hagan,** *American Foreign Policy: A History since 1900* (D.C.Heath & Company, 1991) (Chapters 8 - 12)

Accessible studies with a stimulating biographical slant upon Wilson and Roosevelt include: **Robert Ferrell,** *Woodrow Wilson and World War I* (Bloomington Press, 1985) **T.J. Knock,** *To End All Wars: Woodrow Wilson and the Quest for a New World Order* (OUP, 1992) **Robert Dallek,** *Franklin Delano Roosevelt and American Foreign Policy 1933-1945* (OUP, 1979) **Frederick Marks,** *Wind Over Sand: The Diplomacy of Franklin D. Roosevelt* (University of Georgia Press, 1988) The latter two works take opposing viewpoints on Roosevelt's conduct of foreign relations. Dallek offers an elegant but not uncritical defence whilst Marks offers a refreshingly sharp, albeit flawed, critique.

Among other outstanding recent scholarly contributions to our understanding of American diplomacy and relationship with the rest of the world in this period are the following works: **Daniel M. Smith,** *The Great Departure: The United States and World War I, 1914-1920* (2nd edition, Random House, 1979) **Lloyd Ambrosius,** *Woodrow Wilson and the American Diplomatic Tradition. The Treaty Fight in Perspective* (CUP, 1990) **Warren Cohen,** *Empire Without Tears: America's Foreign Relations 1921-1933* (Columbia University Press, 1987) **Akira Iriye,** *The Origins of the Second World War in Asia and the Pacific* (Longman, 1987) **Waldo Heinrichs,** *Threshold of War: F.D. Roosevelt and American Entry into World War II* (OUP, 1988) **Warren Kimball,** *The Juggler: Franklin Roosevelt as Wartime Statesman* (Princeton University Press, 1988) **Gaddis Smith,** *American Diplomacy During the Second World War* (2nd edition, McGraw Hill, 1985) **Robert Maddox,** *The United States and World War II* (Westview Press, 1988). At whatever level you are studying you would profit from engaging with the ideas and evidence contained in these books.

Sources on 'The USA and the World 1917-1945'
Thomas G. Paterson (ed.) *Major Problems in American Foreign Relations Volume II: Since 1914* (D.C.Heath & Company, 4th edn., 1993) Chapters 2 to 7 of this book contain a range of contemporary documents and selected essays by historians on successively: United States entry into the First World War, The Treaty Fight in the Senate, Diplomacy in the 1920s, Roosevelt, Isolationism and the Second World War, the Wartime Alliance, and the Origins of the Cold War.

Index